don't
kid
yourself!

ROY L. SMITH

don't
kid
yourself!

 ABINGDON PRESS

New York • *Nashville*

DON'T KID YOURSELF!

Copyright © MCMLVII by Abingdon Press

Library of Congress Card Number: 57-5280

The sermon "What's Going On Here?" appeared in
Church Management, April, 1956, and is reprinted,
slightly revised, with the permission of Church Management, Inc.

SET UP, PRINTED, AND BOUND BY THE
PARTHENON PRESS, AT NASHVILLE,
TENNESSEE, UNITED STATES OF AMERICA

preface

THE idioms of a language are among its most interesting forms of speech for the simple reason that they represent the efforts of plain people to express their ideas effectively, unrestrained by the purists. A discerning listener soon discovers that some very profound wisdom goes about in the disguise of slang.

A brief excursion into the dictionary discloses the fact that much of the slang of yesterday, or even the day before, has become the accepted speech of today. Soon after the turn of the century, for instance, the word "skiddoo" was on the lips of the people as a popular way of saying "begone!" Now it appears in the best dictionaries and, in defining its meaning, another slang word still older is used—"vamoose!"

Slang—some wit has called it *slang*uage—is the growing edge of the language. Someone with a genius for graphic expression coins a phrase and tosses it into the hopper of common conversation. There it gets attention, is repeated thousands of times, and in the process takes on a polish that invests it with the authority of common approval. Because it is a convenient wrapping for a widely accepted opinion, it gains currency and perhaps something approaching dignity.

The original phrase may have been the result of a clever effort to express an elusive idea, or it may have represented a highly concentrated bit of conversation; but once it has caught on, it is used as a timesaver by those who are in a hurry, or perhaps as a substitute for original thinking on the part of those who only reflect other people's opinions.

Slang represents a more or less honest effort to express oneself by means of prefabricated phrases. In employing slang millions of otherwise independent people who would not, under any circumstances, stoop to wearing second-hand clothes, nevertheless resort to second-hand conversation. Unthinking slang has the effect of denuding clever expressions of their original meanings, so that otherwise meaningful sayings ripple off our tongues in the form of almost completely unconsidered remarks. This means that they may actually become substitutes for intelligent conversation.

In the course of a visit to New Zealand, I found myself one day in conversation with a famous clergyman of that lovely land who had visited the United States a few years before. "One of my great experiences in your country," he said, "was one Sunday morning when I visited Riverside Church in New York and heard Dr. Harry Emerson Fosdick preach on the theme, 'Who Do You Think You Are?' It was a thrilling sermon, but not the least of my interest in it derived from my great admiration for your American slang. It is so pregnant with meaning."

From that chance conversation came the idea of exploring some of the more suggestive slang which is a part of our everyday speech. Because of its fascinating possibilities it was impossible, of course, to omit Dr. Fosdick's great theme from the exploration, even though the New Zealander's comment included no clue as to what he may have said in the course of his sermon. But the experience of subjecting American slang to serious analysis proved most rewarding, and anyone who is interested in doing so can pick up the thread where these appraisals end, and pursue it almost ad infinitum.

ROY L. SMITH

contents

> *"Then the Lord God
> formed man of dust from the
> ground, and breathed into his
> nostrils the breath of life;
> and man became a living
> being"* —Gen. 2:7

1

who do you think you are?

Dozens of people were lined up before the ticket
window of a theater, waiting their turn to buy admission
to the performance. The show was not scheduled to start
for thirty minutes, and certainly it would not begin until
all were in their seats. Everyone, however, was restless. No
one really needed to be concerned, but everyone was in a
hurry to begin waiting inside.

A rather dignified gentleman stepped up to the window,
ignoring the line, and extended an open palm to the girl
inside the ticket cage. Quite evidently she was expecting him,
for she quickly dropped an envelope into his hand, smiled,
and went on waiting on her customers. It was true that the
man had thrust himself in at the head of the line, and it was
also true that others had been waiting, but no one had been
seriously inconvenienced. However, a boisterous chap with a
raucous voice called out, "Hi there, smart guy, who do you
think you are?"

The question was evidently intended to cut the interloper
down to size (again we are indebted to slang); but on second
thought it is a question in which there is deadly seriousness.
It was aimed at a man who was suspected of exceeding his

9

rights, but it is a challenge every person can well afford to issue to himself—"*Who do you think you are?*"

It is, actually, a very old question—one that the philosophers have been asking all through the ages past. An old Hebrew psalmist phrased it admirably when, inquiring of the Lord God, he asked, "What is man that thou art mindful *of him?*" Why should he be the favorite of all creation?

One ancient philosopher is said to have defined man on one occasion as "a two-legged animal without feathers"; whereupon another philosopher plucked a rooster of his feathers, set the bird upon a table in the midst of the assembly, and said, "Behold your man!"

More recently the scientists have been asking the question, "What is man?" and anthropologists, paleontologists, paleopathologists, archaeologists, sociologists, economists, scientific historians, and many more, have come up with their definitions.

It is impossible for us to take the time to hear all the answers, but we can well afford to examine the testimony of at least three. Any of us can listen to others some other time if we are interested, but now some of us may want to furnish our own small answer. The three we are to consider —the materialist, the psychologist, and the Christian—will start us well on our way.

I. *The Materialist's Answer*

It is something of a novelty for the materialist to find himself required to provide an answer. He has spent so much of his time asking questions that he has almost convinced himself, as well as the rest of us, that he is under no obligation to answer. This, he says, is the responsibility of the religious man. But if materialism is to pose as a working philosophy of life, it must answer the same questions religion, or any other system of thinking, is required to answer.

A university sophomore who had been reared in a strictly religious home was discussing his dilemmas one afternoon with the family's pastor. "I think I will have to give up my religion," the boy said. "I have begun to think for myself and to ask questions, and religion does not seem to have the answers."

"What do you propose to be, if you are not to be a religious man?" the preacher inquired, with all proper solicitude.

"I think I will be a scientist," the youth replied. "He deals with facts, with things that can be handled, weighed, analyzed, and classified. He works with principles that can be demonstrated."

"Yes, I know he has a reputation for doing so," the pastor said. "And as long as he stays inside the field he has marked out for himself, he seems to be quite successful. But have you ever taken the time to investigate whether or not he has satisfactory answers for the questions you have been asking of religion?

"You have been asking some very deep and serious questions. And you have a right to honest answers. You may not know it, but your father and your father's father asked those same questions. Those are the problems that have pursued thoughtful men of every century since the beginning of time. They may be very new to you, but they are very old to the race. I know what your questions are, for I asked them at your age. Over and over I wrestled with them. 'Where did I come from? I know how my physical body came to be, but how did I—the basic and essential *me*—come to be? What is life, and what is there in life worth living for? What is the purpose of it all? Does anything make a difference?'

"Those are all perfectly legitimate questions, and you would not be a normal human being if you did not ask them— and many others. But one thing you must remember. If you abandon religion because it has not yet furnished you with completely satisfactory answers, you will not escape them by the simple expedient of becoming a scientist. They will pursue you into your laboratory and insist upon being answered. They will peer up at you from among your test tubes, retorts, graphs, and statistical tables. And before you know it, you will be hounding your scientific superiors for answers. Don't forget that when you become a strict materialist, you will be faced with the same questions that are tormenting you today. By that time, in all probability, their numbers will have greatly increased.

"Unbelief has all the same questions to answer that belief has. Before you abandon your religious faith, make very sure that materialism has the explanations and that they really answer the questions. For instance, compare the answer of the materialist with those religion has furnished your father. When you have them all before you, then make your choice among them. But never delude yourself into thinking that science provides an easy escape from difficult or unanswered questions."

Quite obviously we cannot seek the answers to all the questions the young man was asking, but we can ask at least one. We have not only the right, but the solemn duty to inquire of the materialist, as the raucous-voiced chap did of the interloper, "Who do you think you are?" It is a simple query; but based on the answer a man gives, we can judge his entire philosophy of life.

A professor of chemistry at Northwestern University framed at least one answer for the materialist when he said:

A man weighing 176 pounds lives in a body which contains enough fat to make nine bars of soap, enough iron to make one good-sized nail, enough lime to whitewash one medium-sized chicken coop, enough phosphorus to make a few hundred match heads, enough water to fill a nine-gallon can, and enough sulphur to de-flea one small dog. Figured at current market prices, he is worth about eighteen dollars.

Is that what you think you are?

From a chemist's point of view that may be the answer, but from a plain man's point of view it leaves a very great deal out of the consideration, and that "very great deal" is our finest and best.

William Shakespeare probably sat down to a good dinner of roast beef and cabbage, and then proceeded to write a thrilling scene for his play, *Hamlet.* Richard Wagner likewise probably ate another good dinner, perhaps of *Hasenpfeffer mit Spaetzle und Kartoffel Pfann Kuchen,* and a few hours later composed a mighty climax for *Tannhäuser.* Edvard Grieg quite possibly regaled himself on *Speckeskinke und Fvetkaalhode* and then proceeded to charm the world with *Peer Gynt.* Ralph Waldo Emerson would undoubtedly have chosen a New England boiled dinner and have gone directly to his study to write one of his famous essays. But no one, not even the most convinced materialist, would pretend to explain *Hamlet* on the basis of roast beef, *Tannhäuser,* as the product of *Hasenpfeffer mit Spaetzle und Kartoffel Pfann Kuchen, Peer Gynt* as the result of *Speckeskinke und Fvetkaalhode,* or Emerson's essay, "Compensation," as the fruit of a boiled dinner.

Life is not so simple as that. We do not have the right to expect masterpieces on any dinner-in-the-slot basis. Jesus of Nazareth once said that a man could not make life out of even an abundance of things. There is a vast area of our experience that cannot be explained on the basis of food, and we do not produce the better things of life by the simple process of doubling our food intake.

Modern advertisers sometimes seem to dispute our Lord

in this regard. A nationally circulated magazine was left on the seat of the Pullman when a passenger, with much expensive baggage, got off the train. On the back page there was a beautifully illustrated advertisement and across it an eye-catching line which said, in effect, "Lay our linoleum and have a happy home!"

There's the answer of materialism! *Linoleum!* Whatever your domestic difficulties may be, lay linoleum! If your marriage is going on the rocks, lay linoleum! If your children are developing as disappointments, lay linoleum! If your in-laws are imposing on you, lay linoleum!

The materialist's answer to our question *"Who do you think you are?"* is completely inadequate. It leaves so very much of all of us out of the account. We must go on to some other one for our answer.

II. The Psychologist's Answer

Relatively speaking, the psychologist—like his near-of-kin, the psychiatrist—is a newcomer in the field of human guidance. For his immense contribution to the healthy-mindedness and wholesome living of the race we are all deeply indebted and should be unrestrainedly grateful. But we are posing for him an extremely difficult question when we ask him, *"Who do you think you are?"*

It is not that psychology itself is so new. The great religious teachers of all ages and races have rested their cases on solid psychological principles. The modern investigator in the field has only reduced it to a science and invented—or appropriated—a new and rather impressive vocabulary which he uses in describing the mysterious processes involved.

If we ask the psychologist who and what we are, he may launch out on an extremely interesting description of how we behave as human beings, how we react, and how we arrive at decisions. He will chart our minds, describe

14

our mental processes with remarkable clarity, plumb our subconscious and help us see our mental infections, and draw a diagram which seems to make very simple our emotional relationships. He will trace our abnormal behavior to its lair among our forgotten experiences and will warn us against attitudes which threaten to destroy our mental balance. But having thus described us, he will leave the hard core of our question unanswered. He will analyze us in terms of psychoses, neuroses, reactions, frustrations, complexes, tensions, eroticisms, inhibitions, mores, and patterns; but when he has exhausted his mysterious vocabulary, we will return to our original question and ask, *"Who do you think you are?"*

A white-haired desert shepherd sat in the shade of a great rock watching an old ram. The beast's wool was burned brown by the glare of the pitiless sun, as it grazed contentedly on the bitter, brittle, desert grass. As he watched, he wondered—and remembered. Forty years before he had been an heir to the throne of Egypt. As a commander of a military expedition into Ethiopia, he had known the experience of riding at the head of a mighty host of men; as a returning hero, victorious and flushed with conquest, he had known the thrill of popular clamor and the satisfaction of royal approval. However, in a rash moment he had struck down a brutal taskmaster who was beating another human being and, as a consequence, he became a fugitive from justice and a hunted man.

As he watched the old ram, his mind was filled with memories of cheering multitudes, of the extended scepter of a mighty monarch, of panoply and power. And he asked questions that no man then living could answer: "What makes the difference between that old ram and me? Why is he tormented by no memories, when mine will not let me rest? What did I gain by striking down the taskmaster?

15

Is there anything, or anybody, in this world who cares when a man does right? What makes anything 'right' or 'wrong'?"

At that moment the old shepherd stood on the most distant philosophical horizon. He was gazing over into a mysterious area of life where the psychiatrist does not venture as a scientist—only as a human being. He was dreaming dreams and resurrection aspirations.

The apostle Paul struck down by a blinding light on the Damascus Way, Martin Luther in the presence of the allied ecclesiastical nobility of the world at Worms, Edith Cavell looking down the rifle barrels of the executioner's squad just outside the city of Brussels, and Bishop Berggrav defying the Nazis from his pulpit in Oslo—all these and an uncounted number of those who have lived and died for dreams dwell as a mighty host just outside the perimeter of any psychological analysis.

You who are sacrificing for ideals, defending justice at the risk of your lives, looking beyond horizons toward the rising sun of the kingdom of God, and living on the power that inflows upon the soul of the man of faith! Let me ask the psychologist for you, *"Who do you think these are?"*

III. The Christian's Answer

The university sophomore who appeared earlier finally said to the preacher, "As a scientific person I want to go back to the beginnings—the first cause."

"And that," the pastor hurried to reply, "is exactly where the Christian starts. His scriptures open with the words, 'In the beginning God . . .' Can any man go farther back than that?"

The aged shepherd, watching the old black ram as it grazed, went back to the beginning. Pulling himself together and standing erect with a glint of the eternal in his eye, he exclaimed, "And the Lord God formed man from the dust of the ground, and breathed into his nostrils the breath of life; and man became a living being!"

The very fact that he asked questions and that the ram did not had the effect of separating the shepherd and the beast by a difference as great as that which intervenes between the living and the lifeless. The fact that he had dreamed dreams, demanded justice, and experienced moral indignation set him apart from all the rest of creation— from all, that is, except other men. For every man is a living being! At this point we begin to get a little light on our question.

The Christian starts from the simple premise that man— every man—was made in the image of God. Man may have arrived at his present state by a long and painful process of evolving, but his beginnings were magnificent. By an act of creation he was launched into the adventure called life on an entirely different level from that upon which every other creature walks.

The first identification of this superior status is the fact that he asks questions. Imagine, if you can, a young ram joining the sophomore and asking: "How did it all begin? What is there in life worth dying for? For what purpose was I born?"

A man and an ox—even an illiterate peasant and a prize-winning ox—will stand on the same spot at the side of the road and watch a dazzling car go by. No questions arise in the mind of the ox beyond the matter of immediate danger. Half a mile down the road the car disappears around the bend. While the ox goes back to grazing, the peasant may start asking questions which continue for the rest of his life. "What made it go? Where did it come from? Who owns it? Why is it that some men can own cars and others do not

17

own even the roofs over the heads? What is wrong with the system that lets one man drive a $10,000 automobile but drives another man to starvation?" When a man begins asking such questions, he becomes dangerous fuel ready for communist fires.

How far and how long such a youth may go in questioning is dramatically illustrated by the case of Abraham Lincoln— a frontier boy fresh from the woods of southern Indiana— as he stood watching a Negro girl auctioned from a slave block in New Orleans. Something very deep stirred within his soul, for he said, "If I ever get a chance to hit that thing, I'll hit it hard." That moment the first tone of the bell was heard tolling the death knell of Negro slavery in America. That day a miracle took place completely outside the field of either the materialist or the psychologist.

A second identification of man's superior status in the scheme of creation is his capacity for moral indignation. Some things are right, and some are wrong. It is not that they are merely advantageous or disadvantageous. The difference goes far deeper than that. Even the Communist who denies the existence of God will concede that. Some things harmonize with the moral order of the universe, and some things outrage it. Some acts and attitudes are those of a good citizen of the universe; other acts and attitudes are those of a moral rebel, a brigand, an outlaw, or a public enemy.

Imagine, if you can, a spirited young horse or a pedigreed pup becoming morally indignant. Or, again, imagine either of them voluntarily offering its life in the defense of a good cause! It is because such attitudes are so common among men that they appear so uncommon among the brutes. But they serve to emphasize the declaration that God created man in his own image—that he breathed into his nostrils the breath of life so that man became a living being.

18

A third identification of man's supreme status in the scheme of creation is the vast significance of his daily conversation, even though he utters only stupid and inane thoughts.

In all of creation there is nothing comparable to human speech. Consider for a moment the magnificence of some of our simplest words. Five hundred times a day, perhaps, we say "I am." And we say it lightly, easily, casually, carelessly, with never a thought for the splendor that shines through these two tiny syllables. But what other creature is able to utter them? True, you can teach a parrot to repeat them, but he does not comprehend them. Behind them stands the sublime miracle of a self-conscious personality. Only a man in whose nostrils there is the breath of life and on whose soul there is the image of God is ever able even to entertain so vast a concept. Yet even little children with their first lisping efforts can say "I am."

Then there follows a mighty torrent of other words equally significant and equally amazing: "I think, I believe, I will, I ought, I must, I can, I hope." And the end of the list no man can estimate!

One more identification of man's significance is his capacity for growth. His first adventure as a builder occurs on the bank of a stream when he constructs a mud hut; but as the day lengthens, we find him raising the towers for a St. John the Divine or the dome for a Taj Mahal.

Even more impressive is the restlessness within his soul. It is a certain divine discontent that will not let him rest until he has created something a bit lovelier, a little more efficient, somewhat more sublime. He spends billions of dollars every year on research because he is not satisfied with what he has done; he spends more billions on universities and cultural agencies because he is not satisfied with what he is. Not content with cracking the atom and tapping the basic sources of the universe's energy, he determines to lay hold on the elemental powers and lift himself up to a level only a little lower than that of God himself. So powerful is the pressure of the image of God in which he is made!

It is with a certain sense of awe, therefore, that we turn to the Christian and ask, *"Who do you think you are?"* And with amazement that defies all language, we hear him reply in the words of John the evangelist: "I am one of those to whom the promise has been made that, if we believe in Jesus Christ, there will be given unto us the power to become!"

There's our answer!

"Who do you think you are?"

One who has been created in the image of God and who has given the power to become!

On one occasion the apostle Paul warned some first-century Christians against the danger of thinking of themselves more highly than they ought. Our Father in heaven is warning us today against the opposite terrible sin of thinking of ourselves less highly than we ought to think, for we have been born to be comrades of the Most High.

He is no egotist who believes himself made in the image of God, who lives as though he were a favorite of creation, who believes he was born with the capacity to hold communion with his Creator.

Just as the bulb was created with the capacity to become a lily, and as the acorn was created with the possibility of becoming an oak, so one who has been born in the image of God has been destined to magnificence as a child of God.

In contrast with all that, who do you think you are? What are you endeavoring to become?

2

what's going on here?

At one of the busy intersections of a thriving Midwestern city there stands a great church, its massive towers forming one of the landmarks of the downtown district. At the rear of the building, opening off a side street, there is an entrance through which one might enter the church office or, by turning in the opposite direction, find himself in the front of the sanctuary in full view of whatever congregation might be assembled.

It happened one Sunday morning that a poor chap, almost helplessly drunk, stumbled down the street and arrived at this side entrance. Quite unaware of where he was or why he was there, he managed to climb the three or four steps and stand just inside the entrance. Pausing for a moment in his bewilderment, he opened the door of the sanctuary, stepped inside, and stood staring into the faces of several hundred people.

It was one of those moments in the service when nothing was happening. No music was to be heard, no one was speaking, and there was no movement. The intoxicated man stood looking at the crowd for a moment and then suddenly called out, "Hello everybody." *What's going on here?"*

The poor fellow's question is a very common one. We may hear it a dozen times a day. But it was never asked more appropriately. Just what happens when a hundred, or a thousand, people come together in the Lord's house on the Sabbath day? What ought to happen? What do we expect will happen?

I. What's the Man Saying?

A Christian worship service is something entirely different from any other kind of human assembly. It is in a church service that we sing a different kind of song, think different thoughts, and fix our minds on different purposes from those which engage our attention at any other time or in any other place on earth. The distinguishing feature of the gathering, at least in a Protestant service, is the sermon.

What constitutes a sermon is a subject upon which there is a wide diversity of opinion. There are those, of course, who insist it should be an exposition of some idea. Others, equally insistent, think it should be a public address in which there is a "lift" for the hearers. Some are unwilling to concede that it is a sermon unless it confirms them in some theological opinion to which they are already committed. Each listener, according to his own definition, expects it to be "down to earth," practical, informative, inspirational, or "spiritual," as the case may be.

A true sermon, however, is a human deliverance in which the voice and judgment of God are heard. One Sunday morning the aged and devout caretaker of a church in a residential section was standing just outside the office entrance when the preacher arrived for the morning service. With fine deference he greeted the clergyman and then, with a twinkle in his eye, inquired, "Good morning, doctor; any late news from God this morning?"

That's it! The pulpit utterance may be eloquent, attractive, interesting, and even pious, but if it does not leave the impression that God has spoken to the people, it may be little more than sanctified entertainment.

A famous judge had listened to a sermon preached by the late Ernest Fremont Tittle, and in describing his experience afterward, he said:

There was a great deal of the thing he said with which I disagreed, and that was what made me uneasy. The preacher made me believe I was listening to God. I had the fear that if I disagreed with the preacher I would, in reality, be disagreeing with God, and that would have been dreadful.

In the last analysis it is this quality which gives a sermon whatever authority it may have. The preacher may quote the church fathers, or he may regurgitate the contents of some scholarly work on theology, but if he does not leave the impression that he is speaking for God, it is not a real sermon.

As a second and very important element, the preacher must never allow himself to forget that the sermon is preached for the benefit of the people, and not for the gratification of the preacher himself. A member of a rather starchy church once said, "We've got a good preacher, I guess, but he is always answering a lot of questions I never heard anybody ask." If the preacher is speaking for God, he will speak to the people.

Had the intruder in the sanctuary been strictly sober, and had he been a thoughtful man, he could not have asked a more searching question of the preacher than when he said, "What's going on here?"

II. Why Are You All Here?

It quite evidently came as something of a shock to the drunken man to find so many people at church; and, it must be confessed, a church full of people raises some extremely interesting questions.

The editor of a metropolitan paper sent one of his crack reporters to inquire of one hundred representative business leaders, "Why don't men go to church?" The result of the inquiry was quite unspectacular. The replies were little more than a variation on the New Testament parable of those who "all alike began to make excuses."

A much more revealing and appropriate question would have been, "Why *do* you go to church?" Even the average service of worship and the usual sermon call for an explanation. Why, for example, should any man subject himself on Sunday morning for thirty minutes to the preaching of another man who may not be as experienced in the business of living, or as well informed on world affairs, or better educated than his listeners happen to be?

It is not enough to say that going to church is a habit to which a certain type of person is addicted. Nor is it quite sufficient to say that "a man needs something to carry him through the week."

Deep within the consciousness of every human being there is something instinctive—as universal as the sense of hunger or the sex instinct. It is what William E. Sangster once spoke of as "a certain homesickness for God." Call it the spirit of reverence, the image of God, or the "intuitive search for the Divine"—it is a basic ingredient of the human soul.

A girl-reporter from one of the papers had just concluded her interview with the pastor of a downtown church and continued to linger as if there were something else on her mind. Finally she said: "I want to ask you a question, and I want you to give me an absolutely honest answer. Did you ever really pray, and did you ever get an answer back from God?" It was very evident that she was deadly in earnest.

"Why, yes, of course I have," the preacher answered. "Hundreds of times."

The little reporter looked at him, her eyes wide with wonder. "I can scarcely believe it," she said. "You see, I was born into a family of atheists. My father hated the Church, and my mother ridiculed religion. I was taught to hold in contempt everything that went by the name of God. But as I have grown older, and especially since I have been in the newspaper business, I have had to attend a lot of religious meetings and conventions, and I have begun to feel that my parents may have been terribly mistaken. I heard you offer a prayer in a meeting not long ago, and it seemed to me something really happened. I heard something in your voice and I promised myself that I would ask you the first time I had a chance. And now you say it is true—that you have really had answers."

As she looked out the window for a long minute, a great wistfulness suffused her face. "It must be wonderful," she said, at last. "I think if I could be really sure of it myself, it would be worth living for and waiting for an entire lifetime. If I could be sure it would happen to me just once in all my life, I think I would be satisfied."

And from the hearer's standpoint, that is what it is! Deep within the souls of men worshiping in the house of God there is a hope that will not rest. Perhaps, this time, they will actually hear God speaking through the preacher, the choir, the soloist, or the service. If they can hear his voice just once, it will be worth a whole year's attendance of church, even if all the other services are fruitless.

It would be disastrous, wouldn't it, to be absent from church the very Sunday God occupied the pulpit?

What a thrilling thing it would have been if the congregation, with one voice, could have replied to the drunken man's question, "We are listening to God!"

III. What's Happening?

The Pentecostal experience of the first-century Christian church was a tremendous event which has had incalculable effects upon human history for more than nineteen hundred years. The New Testament record is very sketchy and leaves a long list of questions unanswered. Some of the language used in describing it is subject to wide interpretation, and we must never forget while we are reading the second chapter of Acts that Luke composed the story sixty years following the occurrence of the event. It would be inevitable that radiant memories would have embellished the report a bit.

The modern church has tried at times to duplicate the Pentecostal experience by reproducing some of the mechanics. There have been those who have thought they were experiencing an Upper Room transformation because they were simulating the tongues, the shouting, and the ecstasies of that birthday of the Christian church.

Perhaps it will help us sense the wonder of the experience if we join those who asked, while they listened and watched, *"What does this mean?"*

The great significance of the Pentecostal experience does not consist of the fact that 120 people spoke in strange tongues and moved about a hall with flames burning atop their heads. A few minutes, or a few hours, and that was all over—whatever it may actually have been. But the world will never recover from the impact of those 120 souls as they emerged from that room and walked through the life of the race as transformed people.

The real meaning of Pentecost was not that flames and tongues had been bestowed upon people, but that men and women had been transformed and made new creatures by the power of God, and that a new spirit had been let loose upon the world, never to leave it. Let anyone who wants to pursue the story a bit further take the time to read Frank S. Mead's exciting book entitled *The March of Eleven Men,* which is the story of the triumphant march of that little company who poured out to travel through the centuries upsetting the old world of evil and of callous injustices.

No, the great thing that happened at Pentecost was not that flames settled upon the heads of men and women, but that they strode out of that room to become flames. It was not that they spoke with strange tongues, but that they went out to preach the power of Christ to redeem men of every tongue. As men who had been born into an evil world and who had become inured to evil, they were suddenly made into new creatures who were never to be the same again.

Suppose some honest soul had answered the intoxicated one, saying, "I do not know what is happening within the soul of any other person, but I have been coming aware of an intimate relationship between my faith and my work during the last thirty minutes. I have discovered that it was as a working man who had never preached a sermon in his life that Jesus was baptized and heard the high praise of heaven, 'This is my beloved Son with whom I am well pleased.' If one working person can win the approval of God with his work, then I propose to be another who will try to do it; and this morning as I have worshiped God, I have worked out an agreement to that effect. I will be a better worker, and God will lay his blessing upon me accordingly."

Suppose some conscience-stricken worshiper in response to the intruder's question should have arisen to say, "I will tell you what has happened to me during the last twenty minutes. I have become aware of the fact that, though I have been making money out of my factory, I have not been making men out of my workers. As one of the leading citizens of this community, active in many good works, I have been concerned with making goods and not with building the kingdom of God. But something has happened to me this morning. And tomorrow morning, when I sit down at my desk at the factory, the institution will have a new manager—an entirely new one."

Or, suppose again, some young man with the bloom of youth upon his cheek and a strange light in his eye should arise and say, "Within the last half hour I have heard the voice of the Eternal, and I have answered with my life."

Even at the risk of monotony, let us suppose one more should have arisen to say, "I came to the house of the Lord an hour ago, my soul filled with terror. The load I have to carry tomorrow seemed more than my powers were equal to bear. The road over which I shall have to travel will be strange and new. But within the last ten minutes I have heard a voice saying, 'Lo, I am with you alway even unto the end of the world.' And now my fears are gone; I will not be afraid."

Even the soul of a drunken man might have been stirred, and he might have been inspired to hope that he, too, could be freed from the curse that was damning him, body and soul.

IV. What Did He Hope Would Happen?

The story is told of a young preacher who went one Monday morning to call on the great Charles M. Spurgeon. In vast humiliation the young man confessed to having failed in his pulpit the day before; in deep contrition he asked for prayers and, if possible, some explanation for his failure.

"What did you preach about, my boy?" the famous evangelist-pastor asked, his voice very tender.

The young man timidly outlined his sermon, sketched in one or two of his most effective illustrations, and concluded with his oratorical climax. While he was speaking, the eyes of the older minister were narrowing. As the report came to an end, Dr. Spurgeon exclaimed, "You surely did not expect to convert anyone with that kind of a sermon, did you?"

"No sir, I guess not," the young man replied.

"Then that is exactly why you did not. You must go into your pulpit with great expectations if you hope for even small results," and the veteran was quite serious.

Suppose in answer to the drunken man's question someone had replied, "We do not know exactly what has happened in the souls of others here this morning, but we can tell you what we have earnestly hoped might happen.

"We have hoped that our minds might be opened and that we might be able to welcome new truths to displace old prejudices. We have hoped that this hour might have marked the time when old envies and jealousies were abdicated. We have prayed God to forgive us for shutting our ears and our hearts against the truth which he has made so very plain to us.

"We came to the house of God this day with the great hope that we who have sought comfort might be aroused to go out into the world as comforters. We have learned that the strength of the Church does not consist of the hosts of those sick saints who gather on the Sabbath day seeking for strength to get them through one more week, but lies in the effective force it can put into the field to battle against entrenched wrong and militant evil.

"We came to the house of God as soldiers to a conference on strategy. We have heard our marching orders and have accepted our assignments.

"As crusaders in behalf of righteousness and the doing of the will of God, we have taken counsel together; and tomorrow morning we will go into the markets, the count-

29

ing houses, the classrooms, and the highways of this community, there to carry out and to declare the purposes of
God, indifferent to the seductions of evil with which we
may be surrounded.

"We have hoped that, as a result of this morning's hour
of worshiping together, some of us might be able to see a
little further around the world, feel a little more keenly
some of the hurt of mankind, look with a little more kindli-
ness on some of those who differ from us in color and
stature. If we came to this sacred place pitying ourselves,
we are now praying God that he may go with us as we offer
our sympathy to the needy world outside.

"We have hoped that, when this hour was done, justice
would have a few more defenders, honor would have a few
more devotees, and Jesus Christ would have a few more
witnesses for the defense.

"We came in the hope that we might hear some sure
word concerning the judgments of God, the concerns of
our heavenly Father, and the tasks to which we are to be
called this week.

"Your question deserves an honest answer, sir, in spite
of your condition. These are some of the things that might
have been happening here; and had you been in a condition really to hear the voice of God, a miracle might have
taken place inside your befuddled mind. None of the things
of which we have spoken are front-page stories, few of them
are spectacular, and no more than a few of them would
ever appear if we did not call your attention to them. But
in terms of the kingdom of God, they are eternal."

If such an answer could have been honestly and truly
given to the intruder, it would not have made much difference who the preacher was that morning, or who sang
the solo in the anthem.

It would have been an hour in which the presence of

God became crystal clear, and few would ever have stopped to consider whether they had heard a good sermon or not.

At least one person who was present said it was that kind of a service, but the question will not down.

"What's going on here?"

3

make mine the same

THERE is no more interesting section in any newspaper than that one in which the readers express their own opinions. It is true, of course, that these lay editorials sometimes fall short of being literary gems, and they may not always make important contributions to the discussion of public issues. But they have at least one very important merit—they are usually quite independent. That, perhaps, is the reason why they are so refreshing.

We may have our suspicions that the business office of the paper dictates its editorial policy, but it is perfectly evident that the vox-pop contributors suffer no inhibitions. Every editorial office which takes any pride in its journalistic ethics allows the readers to dispute the editorial opinion, even when the contradictions become vigorously critical. This is one of the glories of our democratic philosophy.

Nowhere does the difference between a democratic society and the totalitarian state appear more striking than in this willingness to allow the dissenter to speak his piece. A reader's column, open to honest and brave criticism, is inconceivable in a newspaper published in a police state. It could be fatal to such a state if a free expression of dissenting opinion were to be allowed. The one hope of survival for any totalitarianism depends upon a strict policy of thought control.

By the same token, the right to hold and express an independent opinion in the field of religion is the glory of Protestantism. Between the Roman Catholic doctrine of an infallible church, and the Protestant doctrine of the sanctity of the individual conscience, there is an astronomical distance.

It is a basic principle of our faith, as Protestants, that the Holy Spirit deals directly with the individual, guiding him in his reasoning, his intuitions, his moral judgments, and his spiritual quests. If any man is to keep faith with the Divine, he must first of all be honest with himself.

It is inevitable, however, that there shall be differences in moral judgments. That which appears unquestionably right to one person may appear unquestionably wrong to another. What appears to the majority to be wise and good may appear stupid and evil to the minority. But, according to all the principles of our democracy, it is the right of the minority to contend by all legitimate means in behalf of its judgment.

In reciting the events of Jesus' last night with his disciples, Mark describes that tense moment when Peter was warned about his impending collapse. It was so shocking a prospect that the old fisherman exclaimed, "If I must die with you, I will not deny you." Then the evangelist adds, concerning the others, "And they all said the same."

Watch a crowd of teen-agers station themselves on the stools at a soda fountain, and listen as they debate the weighty issue of what to order. At last one of the youngsters, just a little more decisive than the rest, calls out, "Gimme a coke!" Then listen to the others chorus, "Make mine the same."

In the matter of popular styles in clothes, automobiles, books, gossip, politics, television, manners, and morals, their parents sing the same chorus, *Make mine the same!*

I. The Sin of Being Different

There is nothing more dreary in our modern life than the monotony of the popular clamor. We are all expected to see the same pictures, read the same books, adopt the same styles, exchange the same gossip, shout the same slogans, recite the same creeds, vote the same party ticket, and become excited over the same sensations.

Someone has compiled a series of specifications by which we are indexed as liberals or conservatives, isolationists or one-worlders, fundamentalists or modernists, progressives or reactionaries, socialists or free-enterprisers, New Dealers or old-fashioned Americans. Once we have been labeled, we are expected thereafter to think, judge, talk, vote, and perform according to the pattern to which we have been assigned. And woe unto the individual who, resentful of being thus classified, undertakes to be different.

There is something just a little terrifying about the way certain self-appointed individuals make themselves the guardians of public opinion and undertake to punish those who deviate in any way from the line of thought or action approved by this or that "patriotic" organization. Let a thoughtful man offer a protest against a social or an economic danger, and immediately he stands in danger of being labeled as a Communist or at least as a fellow traveler. Let another man come up with a few disconcerting questions concerning the scriptures, and he at once becomes a "modernist," if not an "atheist." Let still another crusade for better housing, and he is called a New Dealer. Let him issue a warning against the depredations of the liquor traffic or against the mounting menace of alcoholism, and he becomes a "prohibitionist."

We have coined an entire vocabulary designed to damn by designations.

There is nothing more dangerous than the tyranny of the majority. Scientific studies have shown, for example, that the individual who really enjoys the taste of alcohol is very rare. If the liquor business depended upon any natural taste for promoting its wares, it would go into bankruptcy overnight. Most of the drinking done in America is unquestionably the result of social compulsion, from which the drinkers are afraid to declare their independence. By exactly the same process of social pressure we have enslaved our wives and daughters to nicotine. Only in the rarest of instances would otherwise sensible women expose themselves to the hazards, inconveniences, and enslavement of cigarettes, with the attendant incidence of increased danger of lung cancers, if it were not for the fear of being called fuddy-duddies.

Psychologists assure us that the lives of literally millions of moderns have been reduced to something like madness by the senseless fear of being different. We wear atrocious hats, painful clothing, and clashing colors because they are the vogue for the moment. We read books that are an insult to decency, we sit through plays that are moronic and movies that are morbid, for no better reason than that they are the "most talked about of the month."

As a Christian and as an American, I rise to protest against all this deadly, sordid, and senseless business. I refuse, for example, to be listed as either a modernist or a fundamentalist. I insist upon my right to be a conscientious follower of Jesus Christ, guided by such facts as may be brought to light by a careful and scientific study of the scriptures, and directed by the personal intervention of the Holy Spirit. I cannot conceive of my Lord taking a neutral position on any moral issue, and I therefore propose to follow his leadership in any case where I become convinced as to what his judgment is. I refuse to judge any man, or be judged, by labels that have been pasted on us by self-appointed judges of orthodoxy.

By similar logic I refuse to be listed as either a radical or a conservative in politics or economics. My government has followed me to the four corners of the earth with defenses and concern, for which I am more deeply indebted than I shall ever be able to repay. The American way has provided me with those opportunities which have made me the envy of three fourths of the inhabitants of the globe, and I can think of no greater blessing that could be conferred upon all mankind than that our democratic pattern should become the way of life for the whole world. But neither the American Government nor the American way has any right to rob me of my individuality or to force upon me any conformity that violates my conscience. I propose to support both with everything I have when I think they are right, but I reserve the privilege of opposing with all my might whatever I think is morally wrong in them or in conflict with the ideals of Jesus Christ.

II. Our Debt to the Independents

In asserting my moral and spiritual independence, and in calling for independent judgment and action on the part of my fellow Americans and brother Christians, I have excellent apostolic precedents. The apostle Paul, in writing to the Christians in Rome, exhorted them saying, "Do not be conformed to this world" (12:2). What he actually said was, of course, "Do not let the pagan mind make up the Christian mind."

It has been the readiness of the Christian to be different and to think differently that has provided us with whatever emancipation from paganism we have achieved. It will be our readiness to be different that will open for us the gates of moral, economic, political, and spiritual salvation, and will

36

prevent us from doing any of those things which reduce life to a series of sham.

It was a Christian priest—Telemachus by name—who struck the death blow to the hideous gladitorial combats throughout the Roman world. Leaping into the arena and holding aloft a little Christian cross, the bravehearted man of Christ demanded that the bestial show should stop. Though the blood-mad multitude shouted him down and Roman guards ran him through with many lances, his spirit arose undaunted from the bloody sands, invaded the royal palace, and, standing that night by the silken bed of Caesar, denied him sleep or rest until he had covenanted within his heart to issue the decree which would end the whole barbarous business. One wonders what Telemachus might do at a modern prize fight in which two of the gentry with cauliflower ears beat each other into near insensibility for the entertainment of the cash customers, among whom there is apt to be found a considerable company of Christians afraid to be different from the contemporary world.

It was a little English woman—a Quakeress named Elizabeth Fry—who determined, after visiting a loathsome prison, to be different. Thereafter, in her gentle and irrestible Quaker manner, she haunted the legislative halls, British officials, and the public conscience until prison reforms became popular and an entirely new era was ushered in.

It was a quiet-mannered, intensely honest, and undaunted French Catholic layman who defied the medical and scientific authorities of his time and revolutionized the whole philosophy and practice of medicine. But through many years Louis Pasteur, now honored and revered, paid an exorbitant price for his independence in the form of ridicule, misrepresentation, and near poverty.

A rugged preacher of righteousness stood in his pulpit in historic old St. Giles' Cathedral in Edinburgh and defied the entrenched authority of the Scottish crown in behalf of the conscience of Scotland. John Knox lived in a very small house on High Street, but he enjoyed a great outlook on life and truth. As a result, the power of a spiritual tyranny was broken and the soul of the Scots was set free to worship.

An heroic and indomitable little priest of the Established Church of England named John Wesley—ridiculed, ostracized, and held up to public contempt by the ecclesiastical authorities of his day—was responsible for a revival of religion throughout the British Isles which, according to learned historians, "saved England from a French Revolution."

In a Methodist meetinghouse a young man came into a Damascus Way experience but, because he insisted upon being different from the Methodists, found the doors of the fellowship closed against him. William Booth, however, was not a man to be daunted by difficulties, and as a consequence, we have today the Salvation Army with its program of good works girdling the globe. Had the Salvationist been content to say the same thing, do the same thing, and be the same thing as all the other Methodists, he might have lived and died as an effective and beloved parish pastor, but the world would have been vastly the loser.

And what shall we say of Albert Schweitzer, Toyohiko Kagawa, Cardinal Mercier, Muriel Lester, Sister Kenny, Sherwood Eddy, Kirby Page, Father Flanagan, Rabbi Stephen S. Wise, and an almost interminable list of others just as courageous and daring who, moved by the spirit of the living Christ, have borne their testimonies in unconventional ways and have reflected the love of God upon the world.

III. The Modern Call for Independent Thinkers

There is a mounting call in this, our day, for Christians who are courageous enough and consecrated enough to live above the level of the crowd.

It is usually easy to declare our independence of some far-distant tyranny. Young people, for example, get a certain thrill out of declaring their independence of their parents. It gives them a feeling of maturity and distinction. But it is an entirely different matter when they attempt to declare their independence of their college fraternity or the social set of which they are a part. Let them try to refuse to drink when they are out of town attending a football game, especially if their team has won and everybody is celebrating. Let them try to live above the sophistication and cynicism which are characteristic of so much of our modern college and university life. Let them dare to declare their faith in their classroom in the face of some doctor of philosophy upon whom the varnish is not yet dry. Ah! That takes real courage! And that is what I mean by being really different.

It is relatively easy to wage war on Communism in the average American community, when we do not know a single Communist by name, when we live safely behind a barricade of common stocks and tax-exempt securities, and when we go to sleep every night on the right side of the tracks. But it is an entirely different matter, this question of fighting Communists, when we find it necessary to engage in a war on those industrial conditions in our modern life which provide fertile ground for Communist indoctrination.

It calls for courage of the highest order to endorse unpopular causes that are designed to provide justice for the exploited, when those causes are opposed by the socially respectable, the economically powerful, and the politically influential. But that is a part of the role I am calling on Christians to play when I warn them that they must be prepared to be different.

It is relatively easy to accept the vows of membership in a Christian church and pay one's weekly pledge to its support.

It is rather comfortable to sit in one's pew on the Sabbath day and listen to music that is inspiring and a sermon that is reassuring. It gives one a sense of social respectability to be able to point to one's church membership as an evidence of good character and good citizenship. But it is an entirely different matter to refuse liquor at a fashionable dinner party, keep the Sabbath day holy in the midst of a secular society, and take a stand for justice in the face of the respectable people of the town. It calls for the utmost in domestic purpose and discipline, for example, to maintain a family altar in these days of disorganization. But these are some of the things I mean when I speak of being different.

The apostle Paul, in writing to the Corinthian Christians, used an extremely graphic phrase. In trying to make them realize their responsibility in the midst of a pagan society he said, "We are the aroma of Christ" (II Cor. 2:15). If there was to be any of the fragrance of the Lord Jesus in the most wicked city of the ancient East, that little handful of nobodies would have to supply it.

If there is to be any redemption of modern life, any transformation of social character, any salvation of society, Christians must become the channels for the divine power that is to work the miracle. To be such, they must be different. Even God cannot redeem such a world as ours except through the medium of redeemed men and women—different from the ungodly that are of this world.

IV. The Creed of the Different

To be a consistent and triumphant Christian, one must have a faith that is both logical and creative. It is easy to declare our opinion that there is a God, and that Jesus of Nazareth was "the Word become flesh and dwelling among us." However, it is an entirely different matter to stake our lives and our living on a confidence that the God whom

Jesus revealed will support us in our defense of the right and in our defiance of the wrong.

Faith is much more than an intellectual judgment. It is an attitude of mind and heart which prompts us to act as though our faith were justified and to live as though the thing we believe is true.

I believe in a God of truth, justice, morals, mercy, and love. I believe he is actively allied with every good cause, every effort that is aimed at the support of justice, and every attitude of mind that represents his preferences.

I believe I can count on him to support my efforts to establish justice, maintain the truth, and deal equitably with even my enemies.

I believe the ultimate victory is pledged to those who are right, those who administer life with love, and those who take up the defense of the defenseless and exploited.

I believe in a risen Christ and, because of that belief, I am convinced that the same God who brought Jesus from the grave will bring victory out of my defeats whenever I am approved of God.

Knowing that the Father of my Lord is my ally, I can be different without being afraid, I can stand alone and still be in the majority, I can continue serene when the tides of victory seem to be running against me.

Confident in the alliance of God, I will stand my ground when others are all saying the same thing.

There are many times when, in good conscience, I find it utterly impossible, immoral, and unchristian to say, "Make mine the same!"

4

how are you doing?

Two farmers chanced to meet quite unexpectedly in front of a little crossroads store and greeted one another cheerily with a question that is commonly current in many sections of the country. Extending their hands to one another they exclaimed, almost in unison, "Hello there! How are you doing?"

It is a friendly greeting which began in solicitude but has ended up as a platitude.

No one really asks it in any serious way, although there are those who accept it literally and immediately launch out on a detailed report of symptoms—what someone has called an "organ recital." It is, however, a serious question and deserves a serious answer.

How are you doing?

There is an Old Testament story from the early years of Israel's history which illustrates the point exactly. Most of us heard it many times during our childhood, and some of us can still remember the strange tingles that raced up and down our spines as we imagined the giant Samson, bound hand and foot, being set upon by his enemies while Delilah, his false paramour, cried out in mock alarm, "The Philistines are upon you!"

Four times the swashbuckling, carefree, and self-confident

superman was warned. Three times he escaped his enemies by a miracle. But at last there came a time when he was really "as other men."

In every man's life there come those times when simple honesty and common sense require that he take stock of himself and of his life. It is so easy to become the victim of disastrous tendencies at the very moment we think all is well with us.

The engineer of a Santa Fe train pulled out of the station in Los Angeles headed for San Diego, completely confident that he was entirely competent to handle his train. Four miles out the engine overturned while going seventy miles an hour on a curve designed to stand up under a strain of fifteen miles an hour. Ambulance crews dug the bodies of twenty-nine dead and more than a hundred injured out of the wreckage—the worst disaster in the history of the railroad. At the coroner's inquest it was revealed that almost a year before the engineer had undergone a thorough medical examination, but that in the time that had elapsed, he had undergone a deterioration of nerves as a result of which he had blacked out for fifteen critical seconds while sitting at the controls. The tragedy had occurred just when he should have been applying his brakes and slowing his train down.

In view of the seriousness with which life confronts us, and the pressures of life under which we live in this high-speed world, we shall be wise if we check ourselves from time to time with the countryman's question, *"How are you doing?"*

I. How Are Your Reactions?

The explanation of the engineer's tragic mistake, offered first by the engineer himself and substantiated later by the doctors, was that he had become unconscious for a few fatal seconds. It had not been necessary for him to be thus

43

from the beginning of the trip. One quarter of a minute of insensibility when his train was traveling at high speed on a low-speed track was all that was needed to cause the disaster.

One of the first tests to which we are subjected in the doctor's office is a series of thumpings and gentle blows designed to show the condition of our reflexes. How do we respond to certain stimuli? Upon the answer to that question rests the decision of the physician as to whether or not we are in good condition. It sometimes happens that the first intimation we have that all is not well comes when the doctor discovers something abnormal, or subnormal, as a result of this simple investigation.

God gave each of us certain instinctive reactions at the moment of our creation. Deep within every human being there is something holy that revolts against injustice, falsehood, indecency, and deception. Call it what you may—self-respect, instinct, or the image of God in which we are made—there is a divine something in us that cries out in protest against the sight of one man, or one class, imposing upon another man or another class. It despises that which is false, that which pretends, and that which connives; it looks with loathing on anything that defiles, debauches, or defrauds.

We are dealing at this point with the very essence of life. Nothing is more holy or more human. It is from these spiritual reflexes that we learn the pattern which sets man apart from all the rest of creation. Other creatures will defend themselves, but man is the only one who will defend a cause; other animals will protect their young, but man is the only one who will die for another's young. It is his readiness to maintain morals, to strive for the achievement of an ideal, to die for a dream, and to sacrifice for a great purpose that makes man not only different but magnificent.

If we are to answer the question "How are you doing?"

44

honestly and accurately, we shall have to examine our spiritual reflexes.

How do we react in the presence of injustices? Does a great cause stir anything deep within us? Are we more concerned about things to live *for,* or things to live *on?* For which would we make the greater sacrifices—to *be* something or to *own* something? For what would we be willing to suffer more—our social position or our personal integrity?

Which causes the deeper pain—the loss of possessions, or the lowering of our sense of honor?

Does the sight of indecency shame us, the report of lewdness disgust us, or the recital of smut nauseate us?

It came as a terrible shock to one young woman who had been reared in the midst of social graces and Christian culture to discover one day that she could listen to profanity and obscenity without cringing and that she could laugh at the maudlin antics of a drunken woman at the office party. "I suddenly realized," she said, "what polite paganism was doing to me."

II. How Is Your Heart?

No physician would consider the possibility of certifying a man for a life-insurance policy without having examined his heart.

When the news that President Eisenhower's heart had failed him was first broadcast to the nation, long lines of patients began to form inside the reception rooms of doctors everywhere. Anxious people who had not previously given the matter more than passing attention now became greatly concerned. "I examined the hearts of more people during that first week following the announcement," one physician said, "than had come to me in almost a year previously. The president's collapse suddenly made everyone aware of the fact that he had a heart, and that it might give way on him."

There is, however, a much deeper meaning implied in the phrase "heart trouble." The ancients used the word "heart" to mean all one's emotions, good impulses, and idealism. When the Hebrew proverbialist exhorted his fellow man: "Keep thy heart with all diligence" (Prov. 4:23 K.J.V.), he had in mind that inner citadel of one's personality from which all one's attitudes, dreams, ideals, and purposes flow.

It is inside this "inner self" (to use a modern's phrase) that the character and quality of one's whole life are determined—whether we are going to be law-abiding persons or rebels against society; whether we are to prey upon our fellows or live at peace with our neighbors; whether we propose to be social assets or liabilities; whether we are to be secular or spiritual in our interpretation of life.

The question, then, of the condition of our hearts is a question concerning the total meaning of life and our response to it.

What is life as it is lived today doing to us? What effect is it having on our hunger after righteousness and our thirst for God? What kind of people is it making out of us? What is it doing to the image of God in which we were created?

A gracious woman who had been a member of an evangelical church for at least thirty years remarked one day, at the meeting of the missionary society, "I'm tired of hearing about all the troubles of the world. I'm bored stiff by these stories of starving children, broken homes, refugees, and juvenile delinquency. I have troubles of my own; and when I go to church, I want to hear something just a little comforting."

That is what modern life is doing to one woman. It was boring her with the daily recital of its troubles!

"I'm tired of hearing our preacher beg for money," said a layman who fared sumptuously every day. "They take a collection every time I go to church. Why can't the rest of the world do something for itself?"

That is what modern life is doing for a large section of the world—producing paralysis of the heart, so that the frequent report of a great opportunity with which the Church is confronted produces nothing more than impatience.

Two men were leaning over the stone parapet that stood on the edge of a freshly cut canyon at the bottom of which a construction gang was laying a track. A well-dressed man was scrambling up out of the ditch, picking his way with some difficulty up the steep and loose bank. As he emerged near the two onlookers, one of them inquired, "What have you got down there, my friend?"

The well-dressed man did not so much as pause to look back, but hurried to his waiting car and, as he did so, called to his questioner, "A bunch of Dagos laying steel for the Milwaukee Railroad."

A minute or two later another man came lumbering up the side of the canyon, this time a heavily bronzed individual who might have been a foreman. As he arrived at the top of the excavation, the onlookers greeted him with the same question: "What have you got down there?"

He paused for a moment at the edge of the embankment, looked down on the busy scene, and replied: "About 120 souls, I would say."

And that was what railroading had done for two different men who were really different!

III. How Are Your Eyes?

A story is told of Dennis Hanks, a cousin of Abraham Lincoln, who as a twelve-year-old boy had shared the rigors and privations of frontier life in southern Indiana with the Lincoln family. Questioned in his old age about the conditions under which the great emancipator had grown up, he said,

"Well, we lived just like the Indians did, 'cept we talked politics and religion."

In spite of the dire poverty, the grim necessities, and the unending hazards and isolation of the Indiana woods, the Lincolns and the Hanks saw something in life just a little more expansive, more idealistic, and more creative than anything their wild neighbors saw. Theirs may have been a bigoted type of religion, and their politics was undoubtedly primitive and uninformed, but both interests were infinitely removed in splendor and concept from anything the Indians knew.

No man has answered the question "How are you doing?" until he has reported honestly on his eyes—on his ability to see the essential and underlying facts of life clearly and accurately.

Optometrists, in testing our eyes, use an interesting chart consisting of a wheel, each spoke of which is a series of black parallel lines. The person with defective vision is asked to tell the examiner which of the spokes look the blackest, and then the lenses are shifted until all spokes appear the same. Normal vision requires that all spokes shall appear equally black.

There is a parable in the optometrist's chart for the man who wants to know the truth about himself. It is a common failure for one to see his rights a little more clearly than he sees his duties, or for him to be more sensitive to his affronts than to the effects of his own bad manners.

The Pharisee whom Jesus compared so unfavorably with the Publican was not really a bad man. The truth is that he was not like other men are. He did tithe, he did live honestly, and he did not extort unlawfully from his fellows. He could defy the world and dare any man to point out any instance in which he had been unjust. But he could not see his bigotry, conceits, and vanities. He suffered from serious eye trouble, so much that even a renegade publican went home justified ahead of him. The tax collector might have been a grafter, a cheat, and generally slippery, but he had at least one crowning virtue. He could see himself for what he really was! The fact that he could see himself accurately constituted the basis of our Lord's confidence that he might be redeemed.

Let it be said to the everlasting credit of the Publican that he never undertook to take refuge in the fact that he was a victim of some kind. He did not complain that he had been "conditioned" when he was a child, that he had grown up on the wrong side of the tracks, or that he had been the frustrated child of domineering parents. Instead, he confessed very frankly that he was a sinner—an original sinner, one whose sin was all original with him. He did not pretend that he had been caught in a web of circumstances for which he was not really to blame and from which he could not escape. Instead, he said, "God be merciful *to me a sinner.*" (Luke 18:3). He offered no alibis and made no excuses. There may have been others who were in some part responsible for the fact that he was a renegade, but he never mentioned them. And he obtained mercy from God because he was merciless in accusing himself of his own sins.

The young Prodigal began working out his own salvation the moment he came to himself and faced the facts of his own life. Read the story again and note how, in spite of the desperate situation in which he found himself, he did not whimper or accuse the world. There were undoubtedly a goodly number of charlatans and tempters—perhaps even some polite blackmailers—in the far country who had taken advantage of the boy's ignorance and credulity to dupe him and rob him of his goods; but he never mentioned any of them, nor did he accuse them. He did not even ask his father to go down into the far country and bring suit against any of them. Instead, he recognized himself for what he had been—a fool—and said, "I will arise and go to my father." Redemption began for him—and he was badly in need of it, in spite of the fact that he came from a good family— when he began to look at himself fearlessly, when he had the courage to look squarely at the facts of life and relentlessly inside his own soul.

News photographers, in getting pictures of athletic events, sometimes shoot their pictures at speeds as high as 1/1000 of a second in order to eliminate the blur that would result from longer exposures. They call it "stopping the motion."

In a swift-moving world such as ours, it often happens that we see life badly blurred. Moral issues become confused, social responsibilities are obscured, motives become inextricably mixed, and spiritual values become vague because of the excessive speed at which we live. Life for most of us is in daily danger of being badly blurred because we are trying to live too fast.

It is appropriate to ask, therefore, as we inquire, "How are you doing?" whether or not we have found a way to stop the motion and get a clear picture of the life we are living. One rare soul once said that every man needed a mountain to which he might retreat occasionally and from which he might be able to look down on the world and get his bearings and perspective. To try to live our modern life without maintaining at least one period for quiet meditation and private prayer, is to invite moral astigmatism and spiritual disaster. No man ever asks himself a more serious question than this: "How are your eyes?"

IV. How Is Your Co-ordination?

One of the tests upon which every physician relies in diagnosing his patients' ills is the sick person's co-ordination.

50

How does his body function as a whole? Can he command his muscles, nerves, and physical reactions so as to be able to rely upon the results? Does he operate as a unit, or as a series of contradictory factors?

The apostle Paul, well aware of the tumultuous forces that contended against each other within him, said, "When I would do good, then evil is present with me." "That which I would do, I do not, and that which I would not, I do." It is a perfect picture of a soul suffering from lack of co-ordination.

We have a name for it in our common speech, and clever authors sell thousands of books which promise to tell us the secret by which to achieve peace of mind and release from our fears.

We say we have an inferiority complex, that we are suffering from inner tensions, or that we are "frustrated." The real trouble is in no way mysterious. A few simple questions, frankly faced, will lead us directly to the roots of our difficulties and distractions.

Have I learned to forgive as I would like to be forgiven?

Do I believe in God, or do I only believe there is a God?

Is my faith an opinion about God, or an intimate attitude toward God?

Have I ever really crowned him Lord of all?

Have I ever accepted my full Christian stewardship for all of life? Do I hold myself responsible to Christ for my every investment of effort, interest, and of possessions?

What is the one basic purpose around which I have organized all my existence? Is it to do the will of God, or is it some way to have my own way?

Are there any rebel habits, passions, desires, or ambitions in my life that have not yet been brought under subjection to the will of Christ?

If prayer is actually the dominant desire of one's life, is

my prayer one that Jesus Christ could endorse to the Father?

The psychologists have a way of talking about an integrated personality. What they have in mind is very much the same as the religious man has in mind when he speaks of the dedicated life. Both the psychologist and the religionist recognize the vast importance of a unified authority, command, or purpose in living. Jesus said, "No man can serve two masters"; the scientist says that the divided personality can very quickly become the diseased personality.

Successful living depends, therefore, upon perfect coordination in which both mind and body have been brought under the control of the spirit. Paul managed to come to that place where he could say, quite confidently, *"This one thing I do."* His was at last the perfectly integrated personality. He was a fully co-ordinated man, all of whose powers could be focused on any phase of life he might choose at any time. There were times when he complained bitterly of the fact that, "The flesh warreth on the spirit," but before he closed his amazing career, he could say very confidently, "None of these things move me, neither count I my life dear unto myself. For to me to live is Christ." (Phil. 1:21.)

No man, asked "How are you doing?" can answer "fine" until he is sure of his spiritual co-ordination.

As a matter of fact, no man can answer so serious a question without thinking profoundly about a number of matters, only a few of which have been suggested in this chapter. "How are you doing?" is a question with some phase of which every honest man ought to come to grips at least once a week!

5

where's the fire?

THE president of one of the big banks of the town dropped the telephone receiver into its cradle, his hand trembling and his face ashen. Looking at his secretary who had been in the act of taking dictation, and with a terrible throaty tone in his voice, he said, "They have just found George dead at his desk—a suicide!"

With that he swung around, arose, and went to the window. There he stood, staring down at the frantic traffic in the street below. A dead silence hung over the room. Finally, in an obviously desperate effort to get control of himself, he turned from the window, went back to his desk, and seated himself mechanically as though he were no more than half conscious of his surroundings.

"It's the pace! It's the pace!" he muttered. "That's the third one in the last month."

Modern life is taking a horrible toll of mankind. Every morning's paper tells the story of some tragedy that has occurred as a result of the killing pace at which we are living and of the mountainous loads we are trying to carry. It is not only among the top executives of big business that the cruel pressure is felt; the plain man on the street shares it in equal measure but at a different level. None of us can escape the perils it entails.

53

It goes without saying that there are vast areas of modern life in which we can take great pride. We have achieved an almost incredible degree of efficiency; our assembly-line techniques have enriched the common man with an abundance of good things which make him the envy of the centuries, so that even the humblest among us enjoy comforts and share in delicacies that were out of the reach of royalty one, two, or three decades ago. Sulfa drugs, antibiotics, prophylactic medicine, and public-health precautions have robbed life of a thousand terrors. Even in a few spiritual areas we have risen almost to the glory level. Never in all the history of mankind, for example, has one great nation shouldered so much responsibility for the world's burden of woe as has been the case in the foreign-aid program of the United States during the last ten years. For all of this, let us thank God!

But it is also true that something deadly has infected modern life. Men and women, literally by the thousands, are cracking up. The psychopathic wards everywhere are overcrowded; doctors say that at least fifty per cent of their patients are suffering from mental maladies which have induced physical disorders; an entirely new science has developed in the field of medicine called "psychosomatics," which attempts to deal scientifically with people who are coming apart at the seams mentally and physically. In the meantime the druggists say that millions of sleeping pills are consumed every night.

In the face of the multiplication of mental maladies, the increasing strain of life, and the mounting tension everywhere evident, serious-minded men are beginning to ask: "How long can the human personality stand the pressure? Is the burden of civilization building up past the point of human endurance?" It is a problem with which psychiatrists, psychologists, physicians, sociologists, industrialists, and educators are profoundly concerned, and one to which they are giving their most careful and scientific attention. It is also a problem to which good religion must give major attention or lose the right to be called good.

A motorist in a speeding car ran through a traffic light, and a motorcycle officer took off after him with a roar. Half a mile or more down the boulevard, he signaled the driver over to the curb. As the policeman dismounted and approached the speeder, he exclaimed, with more than a little irony in his voice, "Hello, my friend. Where's the fire?"

The speeding driver was not drunk, nor had he been drinking. He had been in complete control of his car every foot of the way. But the moment the officer got a good look at his face, he recognized him for what he was—a man consumed by an inner fever. Every fiber of his being was tingling with tension; his speech was crisp and metallic; his fingers grasped the wheel as if they might have been steel clamps. There was a fire, but *it was in the mind of the speeder!*

I. Let's Admit There Is a Fire

The first step in the cure of a disease is to recognize it for precisely what it is—a disease. A vast amount of good medicine has been wasted because of a faulty diagnosis. As a wise old countryman once said, "There are altogether too many people dying in these parts of the wrong disease."

We have with us today a widespread cult of denial composed of those who insist there is no such thing as pain, sin, or fault. Sinners are assured that they are victims; sufferers are told that they need only to "think positively instead of negatively." With a certain superficial glibness, the tortured are instructed to declare in the midst of every painful situation that "all around me is sweetness and light," or that "I am power and life," or perhaps that "every day in every way I am getting better and better."

That there is a vast value in an aggressive faith goes without saying. There is all too much tendency for religious people to assume that they have faith because they hold a correct opinion concerning God, goodness, and life. But a creative faith consists of an aggressive attitude based on a well-reasoned interpretation of the facts. Indeed, no really rational faith ever shuts the eyes of the faithful to any established truth. It holds one ready to face the worst and the most mountainous fact, wide eyed and realistically. It is as irreligious to ignore a fact as it is to deny the love of God.

The increasing prevalence of alcoholism in its various forms and degrees of desperation is striking evidence that fires are burning over a wide area of modern life. Every drinker, no matter how polite or how moderate his drinking may be, drinks with the hope that alcohol may provide him with an escape from the pressures of life. Lacking the necessary inner strength he needs to face the realities of life, he takes refuge in alcohol.

The widespread use of cigarettes is but another symptom of the same social and psychological disease. The smoker smokes for the purpose of "relieving the tension," for "the quieting effect it has on the nerves," or for "the lift it gives." Being unable to find spiritual resources within himself to accomplish these desirable results, he leans on nicotine.

The divorce courts of the nation furnish additional evidence that a frightful fire is burning away the vitals of our civilization. Emotional instability, a complete lack of self-discipline, tensions, mental maladjustments—the complaints and cross complaints are strewn with the evidence.

The first step that good religion requires every person to take in the direction of rehabilitation is to admit that there is a fire—that something is wrong and must be made right. No pastor has ever been able to help in any substantial way until the distressed and distraught person is ready to say, "I'm wrong, and I need help." Alcoholics Anonymous, resting its case upon an amazing experience of success in assisting chronic sufferers, insists at the outset that the alcoholic shall admit that he has come to the end of his rope. The wise pastor, in advising with the sinner, undertakes to help him come to himself before he has gone the limit.

The evangelists of a generation ago made every effort at the outset of their campaigns to "bring the town under a conviction of sin." It was their way of saying that the first thing necessary in any unsuccessful spiritual redemption is to persuade the victim of sin to realize the frightful reality of the malady. As a matter of scientific spiritual prophylactics, it is far better to extinguish the blaze while it is still small, than to wait until it has become a holocaust. Just as it is said, "You can't have a little garlic," so it needs to be said, "You cannot be a small sinner." Sin and fire have at least one characteristic in common—neither is harmless just because it is small.

II. Let's See Where the Fire Is

Someone turned in a fire alarm, but in his excitement located the blaze at the wrong address. The section of the city in which the fire had started being a tangle-town with a maze of diagonals, curving streets, and dead ends, the fire fighters lost their way. They finally wound up in a street from which there was no exit and could not get turned around. In the meantime other equipment arrived until there were enough men and machinery available to extinguish three fires, but no one seemed to know where the fire was.

It is precisely at this point in our spiritual distress that psychology renders its most valuable assistance. It clears away the mental undergrowth and digs down into the well of the subconscious where we have dropped our remembrances. By bringing up old misconceptions and distorted ideas and revealing them for what they are, it enables us to cleanse our minds of infections. Thus the individual is started on his way again in the direction of normal and wholesome living.

At the intersection of two heavily traveled streets in a great American city, there occurred a serious accident in which a fire truck collided with a limousine. One of the drivers was thrown clear of his car and the decapitated body dumped at the feet of a five-year-old boy. The little one ran screaming to his mother in a nearby house. After perhaps half an hour, however, she succeeded in quieting him, and that evening he recited the experience to his father somewhat zestfully but calmly.

Later as a high-school boy he was athletically ambitious but reticent. In spite of the urging of his friends and the team's coach, he always played a waiting game. In college he made one of the varsity teams, but again he played a game that avoided all fierce encounters. Instead, he "took advantage of the breaks." Then came a game when, in a mad scramble, he was rendered unconscious for nearly half an hour.

Upon returning to consciousness, he declared that he was uninjured, that he suffered no pain, and that he was quite himself again. The following week, however, he played an entirely different type of game, being in the midst of every melee and fighting for every advantage. The season ended the next week with a game in which he was the scoring star, and with that brilliant performance he closed his college athletic career. Then it was, in a conversation with his father, that the deep hidden secret came out.

"I never understood it before," he said, "but the sight of that bleeding body when I was five filled me with a terror of being hurt. As a boy I could scarcely endure the sight of blood, and even a small scratch on my hand that drew blood almost caused me to faint a few times. But when I crashed into the boards and awakened to discover that I was uninjured, I suddenly made a great discovery—*I could be hurt without being hurt. And now all my fears are gone!*"

Life for millions of moderns is being reduced to a nightmare by fears which are the result of sins. Contemptible living, accompanied by a profound sense of guilt, produces a ferment within the depths of the soul and in the process produces a series of spiritual infections, including some ghastly fears. For such sufferers the only hope of salvation consists of an inner cleansing of the mind as well as the spirit—one which reveals sin and fears for exactly what they are.

During the years that I served as the editor of a religious paper, I received literally scores of letters from individuals who confessed, sometimes in the most pathetic terms, secret sufferings which resulted from early sins. Some of these were real, but a smaller number were at least partially imaginary. In a few cases near relatives assured me that my correspondents were suffering from actual mental derangements as a result of mismanaging their thinking. Undoubtedly a skilled psychiatrist with a sympathetic attitude toward religion could have restored such sufferers to something like normal attitudes and life.

There come times in the lives of all of us when the most religious thing we can do is to explore our own souls for the purpose of discovering any long-standing grudges, animosities, hatreds, envies, jealousies, or resentments that may be lurking there. Jesus was employing a demonstrable spiritual law which has a solid psychological basis, when he said: "If you are offering your gift at the altar, and there remember that your brother has something against you, leave your gift before the altar and go; first be reconciled to your brother, and then come and offer your gift." Our fathers were religiously right and psychologically correct when they inquired insistently of the penitent whether or not there was anything he ought to make right with his neighbor. The modern psychologist is equally correct in his efforts to persuade his client to "drain his mind completely."

Every resentment we cherish sets up a spiritual infection which has the effect of destroying serenity, peace of mind, and spiritual co-ordination. The doctors have proved that an infected tooth can wreck the functioning of an entire body, and the experienced pastor knows that a bitter and unforgiving spirit reduces an otherwise healthy soul to helplessness.

When Jesus assured his disciples that they must forgive "until seventy times seven," he was not concerned about the welfare of the one who was to be forgiven. Instead, he was prescribing for the one in whose spirit an unforgiving attitude was working havoc. He knew there could never be spiritual peace or effectiveness in that life, or power in that personality, until the contaminating and corroding thing had been completely removed.

There is much merit in the highly popular modern advice to "relax." No mind or spirit can function normally when it labors under any form of self-induced tension. There is, however, a subtle danger in any relaxation which ignores actual spiritual infections. It can happen that, in trying to "forget it all," we are only perpetuating our troubles, much as if we wrapped a boil in a bandage.

When one is aware of the fact that he has sinned and then attempts to thrust the whole matter back and down into the subconscious, he is only preparing his spirit for more suffering. It is not unlike what happens when an infected gland is allowed to distill poison in the blood stream. No sin can readily be forgotten until it is forgiven, without doing the spirit vast damage.

Again our fathers were entirely correct and quite scientific (without knowing how scientific they were) when they insisted that the penitent must confess all. It was their non-technical way of producing a thoroughly scientific result. There can be no permanent or creative peace inside any human spirit until it has been cleansed of all evil moods and attitudes to which it has extended hospitality.

The door of my study was suddenly thrown open one afternoon, and a man and his wife entered, unannounced. I knew them well and esteemed them highly, but I was astonished to have them come in so unceremoniously at such a time of day. I did try to cover my astonishment, however, with a bit of jocularity, as I exclaimed, "Well, well, well! How does it happen that I am honored thus in the middle of the afternoon?"

Without any polite introduction, beating about the bush, or mincing of words, the woman said, "We've come to see you about me!"

"And what is your difficulty?" I inquired, quite aware now that the situation must be serious.

"I am cursed with a devil of jealousy," the woman replied. "For ten years I have made life a hell for this man. I have accused him falsely of every foul and terrible thing. He has been undeserving and he has been patient, but he has come to the limit of his endurance. Unless you can help us, our home is gone, our marriage is on the rocks, and our lives are ruined. It is my fault, and I am the one you must help."

When I had recovered my poise, following this impassioned and brutally frank outburst, I contrived to get the interview started on an even keel. It was not easy, but the final outcome was a thrilling spiritual victory. It was made vastly easier, however, because the woman who proved to be the one actually guilty, was perfectly honest about the whole situation. She knew exactly where the fire was and guided all of us to it without the loss of time or effort.

Complete spiritual honesty was the secret of the speedy redemption of Zacchaeus, the diminutive tax collector of Jericho, who climbed up into the tree to get a glimpse of Jesus as he passed by. The first moment he was alone with the Lord, he confessed he was a sinner, identified his sin, and proceeded to outline a cleansing program for his life. There is a necessary cleansing process which is quite beyond the power of any man to put into effect. It depends upon the direct action of God. But that process never goes into action until the sinner has gone the full limit of his ability, on his own behalf, to cleanse his own heart. As a young bank clerk who had come to that point said, "From here on out I must trust God to make up the deficit."

Blessed is the man who really knows where the fire is, for his redemption is well begun!

III. Let's Put the Fire Out

After we have faced the fact that there is a fire and have identified it, the final step is inescapably plain. We must proceed to put the fire out!

The word of the psalmist which is our text offers the first suggestion. "Be *still*, and *know*."

Spiritually speaking, being still is the most difficult task to which some of us ever assign ourselves because we are so accustomed to associating religious experiences with activity, and have grown so accustomed to praying, "Lord, what wouldst thou have me *to do?*"

Instead of trying to "get away from it all," to find another environment, to associate with different people, or to give oneself in service, we must "take time to be holy." Activity, service, and zeal in good works—all these may come later and doubtless will contribute largely to the re-creation of our lives. But the initiatory rite is *being still*.

Watch the great pianist as he sits down at the piano to begin his master performance. Note how he spends perhaps a full minute gathering poise and bringing every muscle, nerve, and mood under a single mastery. Watch the world-famous athlete as he balances himself delicately, mustering every power of his supple body into a disciplined line. Championships are the result of poise and strictly unified control. As the Negro maid in a great sanitarium said to one of the patients, "I've noticed that it makes all the difference in the world what kind of environments a person's got inside of them." Taking time to be holy is, in its simplest terms, the ordering of one's own soul.

First of all, in that high moment of quiet, let us fix our minds firmly on a simple proposition—God is love. We do not need to argue with our heavenly Father; we are under no necessity of convincing him that we deserve good at his hands. We do not need to remind him of any extentuating circumstances. He knows them, every one, and has them all in mind, and his opinion of us has already been conceived in love. He has already planned well and lovingly for us. Nothing we can say and nothing we can plead can persuade him to do any better for us than he has already planned on doing, for his mind has been made up by divine love inspired by divine forgiveness. Let the magnificence of that prospect take possession of our minds and hearts, and the peace and quiet it will produce will amaze us. We will find the fire burning very much lower.

As the second exercise, let us assure ourselves that the love of God operates on a completely dependable basis. Just as the law of gravity can be relied upon under every circumstance and at every minute, so the law of divine love can be trusted. It is of the utmost importance that we should remember that divine love is orderly—that it is completely obedient to law. When we know the laws of love, we can co-operate to achieve the results of love.

There are those attitudes of mind and heart that result gloriously, and there are those others that result disastrously. Because God designed us as living souls and not as mechanical robots without moral responsibility, he gave us the right to choose. Even God could not love us if our goodness were involuntary. It is of the utmost importance, therefore, that we keep ourselves aware of the fact that when we have chosen our attitudes, we have also chosen the results of those attitudes. This means we can have the kind of life we desire by choosing the attitudes which produce that kind of life.

A young bank officer, tortured by a medley of fears and accusing memories, appealed to his pastor for help. "I am caught in a maze of mistakes." he said. "I don't know what to do to escape."

The pastor proceeded to outline for the young man a very simple program. He was to return to his desk at the bank that very afternoon, sort over his responsibilities, and pick out one thing he could do absolutely right—to make one decision that would be defensible in every way—and see what happened.

Early the next morning the young man called the preacher, and said, "I did it! The thing I did was absolutely right, and it was also pretty difficult. But even God almighty approved of the way I did it. And last night when I lay down to sleep, there came over me a sense of rightness and well-being that I have not known for months. I knew there was still a lot that was wrong, but there was also *one thing that was right!* And with that thought in the front of my mind, I went to sleep in peace. It was wonderful. This morning I awakened refreshed and enthusiastic about my new day."

Day after day the young man repeated the process. Each day he did one new thing that was right, discarding something wrong or deciding against some wrong course of action. Within the space of weeks he was a new man. He now had an accumulation of right things to his credit, and the Holy Spirit of God was bearing a reassuring witness within him.

The third exercise through which one must put his spirit, in putting out the fire, is to assure himself over and over that God is very patient with him.

If anyone questions God's patience, let him stand at the edge of the Grand Canyon, in imagination at least, and try to conceive of the endless ages during which God has been at work carving it out. And if God would take all that time and those pains in eroding a canyon, is it inconceivable that he would hesitate about taking a little more time to carve out a human soul?

Or, if you prefer, stand some night under the stars and try to estimate how long ago it was that God started the ray of light toward you which strikes your eye at that moment. Thousands, even millions, of light-years may be involved. The astronomers say that the light that comes from the farthest star in our solar system started at least four hundred years ago! And there are other systems infinitely removed, still visible to the naked eye.

With all this in mind, repeat those thrilling words of the apostle Paul: "While we were yet sinners Christ died for us!" (Rom. 5:8). He began expressing his concern and solicitude thousands of years ago. How patient he has been!

Ages and ages before we were born, God began preparing our world for us. He taught the flowers to grow and the earth to produce of itself. And when that first weak little cry issued from our infant lips, he had the world all ready to receive us.

This means that he has no intention of giving us up. A

single bit of defiance, some wild oats, and even outright rebellion—none of these things can ever have the effect of discouraging God, even though they may hurt him terribly. "Return unto me and I will return unto you," he says. And the promise is never repealed.

Nourish your spirit on these three assurances, and you will someday discover that the fires are burning lower within your soul. Someday you may discover that they have been extinguished.

The power of inner fires has been made more bewildering, perhaps, because of the theology with which we have surrounded the matter of forgiveness. It is, however, relatively simple when we approach it with a complete confidence in the love and patience of God.

The first thing to do is to identify the fire for what it is. Next we have to approach it as if God could be trusted.

As a young businessman once said, "It helps me straighten out my thinking just to remember that I can trust God to be a gentleman!"

> *"Forgetting what lies behind and straining forward to what lies ahead, I press on toward the goal for the prize of the upward call of God in Christ Jesus."* —Phil. 3:13

6

where do you think you're going?

WHEN the traffic light changed, two swarms of pedestrians flooded out into the street. In the midst of one crowd there strode a tall, spare man who walked with a highly nervous step. There was a grim expression on his face, as though he might be laboring under some great strain. His jaw was firmly set and he looked straight ahead of him, glancing neither to the right nor to the left, and seeing nothing and no one.

Suddenly, almost precisely in the middle of the street, he bumped squarely into a heavy, good-natured individual with whom he was evidently well acquainted, for the fat man called out cheerily, "Hi there, Tom! Where do you think you're going?"

It is one of the unfortunate facts in the life of most of us that someone tosses that very serious question at us almost every day, and we do not hear it. Were we wise enough or clever enough to give it even a few minutes of careful consideration once a week, the beneficent effects would begin to show up in our living within a month. In one of the most critical periods of his spectacular career the apostle Paul, taking stock of himself, wrote to his friends in the distant city of Philippi, saying: "I propose to forget what is behind me, and I will strain forward to what is ahead, pressing on in the direction of the upward call of God."

I. Where Do You Think You Are?

The first fact to determine in answering the question "Where do you think you're going?" is *where you are.*

An old Chinese sage in Peking was proving to be a highly interesting companion, and his collection of ancient astronomical instruments was quite evidently something in which he had taken an extended and intense interest. "There is one difference between your compass and ours," he said, very gravely, and then paused as if waiting for me to ask the obvious question, which I did.

"What is that difference?" I inquired.

"Your compass," the aged man answered, "has four points— north, east, south, and west. But ours has five."

"What are they?" I asked, more than a little curious.

"Well, we have all the points of the compass you have," he continued, speaking slowly, "north, east, south, and west. Then we have one other—*where you are.* No one ever really knows which is north, east, south, or west until he knows, first of all, *where he is.*"

There was a bit of rare wisdom in the old sage's explanation, and in answering the question "Where do you think you're going?" each person must undertake to discover for himself precisely where he is.

Modern life is a torrential thing. On every side we are being importuned by salesmen of gadgets, opinions, ideas, sensations, vitamins, cigarettes, toothpaste, automobiles, and sleeping pills. Someone took a nonprofessional poll of the television programs to which he was being subjected in the course of one week, and came up with the conclusion that at least one half were sponsored by those who wanted to sell him something that would anaesthetize his spirit or fortify him against the speed and strain of spirit by means of drugs, narcotics, or vitamins.

Every alert pastor is familiar with the cases of those parishioners who come to him tense and tired, utterly unaware of the fact that they are losing ground morally and spiritually. So many times they are deluded into thinking that they are succeeding magnificently. Their business is growing, their bank balance is improving, their securities are paying extra dividends, their golf score is in the low eighties, they are being invited to join fashionable and exclusive clubs, and their children are being pledged to swanky sororities and fraternities. But as Dr. Harry Emerson Fosdick describes them in his great hymn, "God of Grace and God of Glory," they are "rich in things and poor in soul."

Literally millions of moderns are on the move. According to chambers-of-commerce figures, approximately one third of all our American families have been uprooted during the last ten years. In some cases the moves have been made only from one section of the city to another, but in others the transfer may have been halfway across the continent. The resulting disturbance of life, habits, standards, morals, ideals, and social solidarity is staggering, some of the most serious effects being registered in the cases of young children into whose lives a great sense of insecurity has been introduced. Schools, churches, scouting organizations, and character-building agencies are unable to serve on anything better than a touch-and-go basis. The turnover in some of our Sunday schools amounts to almost fifty per cent of the total enrollment in a single year.

But our children and youth are not solitary sufferers. Whole families, literally by the thousands, are deteriorating as a result of gypsying. The Church Federation of one American city with a population of more than 1,500,000 estimated there were inside the city limits at least 100,000 persons who had been members of some Christian church "back home," but who had never transferred their membership to any local congregation, and of which 90 per cent must be counted as lost permanently to the church. It is one of the tragic weaknesses of our modern churchmanship that our people do not survive successfully the ordeal of transplantation.

In attempting to determine where we are, as individuals, it will help greatly if we will sit down quietly, ask ourselves a few questions, and answer them with complete candor. Because no one need ever see the answers, aside from ourselves, we can afford to be absolutely relentless in our honesty. Only so can we enjoy the profit the exercise will pay.

Is my religion making any real difference in my life?

Do my prayers produce any actual power?

Am I the real owner of my property, or do my possessions possess me?

Are my present attitudes producing for me the results I really want in my life?

I what respect is my life unsatisfactory, and what can I do to make it different?

If I should suddenly lose all I own, how much would I be worth?

How sure am I of God?

How sure am I of myself?

How much of a disappointment does it take to make me bitter?

Am I a difficult person to live with?

How heavy are the demands I am making on my loved ones?

Can I be trusted to keep my word when the going gets really tough?

Am I the master of my life, or am I the one who surrenders to his difficulties?

Precisely, where am I?

II. Mid-Term Examinations

The schools make use of an extremely revealing device called "mid-term exams." They are an ordeal to which a student is subjected midway in the semester and are designed to show whether or not he is mastering the material offered him. It gives him an opportunity to check up on himself, take stock, and plan his future course. The grade he is given is not final. Instead, it is what might be called a scholastic barometric reading, intended to indicate what kind of weather may be expected just ahead.

If we propose to ask the question "Where do you think you're going?" in any serious fashion and in the hope of getting any constructive results, the first inquiry in our mid-term examination will raise the economic issue. Are we learning to live independently of our possessions? In other words, are we becoming independently rich?

The charge is frequently made that "the Church is always talking about money," and the accusation is well justified. Indeed, that is as it should be. If the Church is to serve as a redemptive agent, it cannot escape the responsibility of talking about money.

Jesus established the precedent in that regard. Long before he ever preached a formal sermon, worked a miracle, or told a parable, he had settled the economic issue, and on the occasion of his temptation said, "Man shall not live by bread alone" (Luke 4:4). Later on in his public ministry in the course of one of his sermons, he laid it down as a basic principle of spiritual living that "a man's life does not consist in the abundance of his possessions" (Luke 12:15). A hurried review of his parables reveals the fact that the vast majority of them consist of teachings related to some aspect of our responsibility for the management of money. No church

71

can be Christian and ignore the profound spiritual problems associated with money.

In my morning paper there appeared the pathetic story of a woman who died, leaving an estate valued at $1,500,000. By her will this huge sum of money was bequeathed to a committee of six citizens of her community which was to distribute it to good causes according to its best judgment. "It has been the great mistake of my life," she had written in her will, "that I have never learned how to give money away."

No one has learned to live well who has not worked out an intelligent and reasonable philosophy of stewardship. No one is really free who is not free from the entanglements of his possessions. Miserliness is not an occupational disease of the rich. The attitude of one toward his wages of $40 a week can be as evil as the niggardliness of another man who handles $400 a week.

A second question in our mid-term examination is very certain to raise the whole issue of our management of life. Are we living according to a plan, or are we the victims of each new day as it dawns? Do we go out to meet life with a victorious spirit, or do we wait and cringe until it sweeps in upon us and overwhelms us? Do we live aggressively as masters, or negatively as victims? If we have a plan for our life, is it adequate? Does it include all the possibilities? Is it sufficiently long range?

A benevolent minded and greatly beloved professor in a famous medical school was engaged in an intimate conversation with one of his students who had just been notified that he had passed his final examinations successfully and was to be awarded the coveted degree of Doctor of Medicine. It was a happy occasion for both of them, and the teacher was aglow with satisfaction.

"And now what do you intend to do?" the teacher asked.

"Well, first of all, I have an internship which will take up my time for the next two years," the young man said, "and after that I am planning on another internship and some graduate work in the field of children's diseases. I am going to be a child specialist, you know."

"That is splendid," the professor said quietly. "I could not imagine anything finer. And after that, what?"

"Well, I am planning on private practice for a while, but eventually I want to have my own hospital. There are several areas in the field that have never been thoroughly developed, and maybe I can make a contribution in one of them. I might even write a book!"

"And after that, what?" And the old professor was quite serious now.

"Well, I suppose I will take my place in the life of the community—run for the school board, serve on the board of directors of some social agencies, or something like that. I'd like to be a good citizen. I'm not too eager to make a lot of money, but I should like to be a really useful scientist."

"And then?" And the old professor was really probing by this time.

"I suppose by that time I'd be getting along in years. I'd like to travel a bit. Maybe I can retire and give all my time to research for the few remaining years of my life."

"Then, after that, what?"

The young man was quite evidently restless now. The conversation had taken a turn for which he was not prepared. But he was not ready to surrender, and so he exclaimed, "Professor, what is there after that?"

"Ah, my boy," the older man said, as he laid his hand affectionately on the youth's shoulder, "that is for you to decide. Actually, I had hoped you might have decided it by this time. But if you have not, it is the next thing on the

73

agenda. You'd better settle it soon, before any complications set in."

The evangelists of our fathers' day had a good deal to say about the Judgment Day. We seldom hear a sermon on that theme in these later times, and that's the pity. Some of us may find it difficult to accept the theology of that earlier day about a burning pit and pearly gates, and that may not be necessary. But it is of the utmost importance that we should occasionally face the stern reality that ultimately we and our lives are to be measured alongside the ideals and principles which Jesus taught. One of our Lord's teachings was that we are citizens of two worlds—that this life is an apprenticeship for another. In the presence of such a situation the most important question any man can ask is the query of the theme with which we began, "Where do you think you're going?"

III. The Upward Call of God

There is something magnificent about man which sets him apart from the universe in which he lives and from all other creatures and things in it. He dreams dreams no other living thing ever knows, and he feels moods and impulses no other creature is ever able to share. It is true, of course, that he is moved by the sex impulse as are also the hog or the ram. He is driven by hunger as are the wolf and the ferret. He contends with fear as do the deer or the rabbit. But he also masters the sex impulse, he disciplines his hungers, and he conquers his fears. As one very wise man once said, "He has all the characteristics of the animal, but he is the only animal that is profoundly aware of the fact that he is an animal, and that it is possible for him to become a better one."

He is capable of being profoundly moved by a sunset, by the music of a rippling stream in the forest, by the approach of a storm, by a cause that is just, and by the sight of a brutal injustice. As a result of the pressure of the universe upon him, he writes poems, paints pictures, creates symphonies, raises altars, explores the infinitesimal, and organizes democratic governments for the purpose of assuring human rights. All these are outcroppings of what the author of Genesis called "the image of God," in which man is made.

We are accustomed to say that we have been tempted by evil desires and passions, but it is an even more common experience to be summoned by the splendid, enticed by the magnificent, and tempted by dreams of the glorious. In the lives of even the most brutal among us there are evidences of the effects of what Paul called "the upward call of God." Pasted on the steel wall of a prison cell occupied by a "lifer," who was doomed to spend all his remaining years in prison for having committed a particularly fiendish crime, we found a picture of a baby. Immediately beneath it was a spray of wild flowers; for within even the soul of a brutalized man there was something holy that would not die.

Beside the highway which runs through Port Gibson, Mississippi, there stands an old brick Presbyterian church surmounted by a slender steeple that stretches up into the blue. Atop the spire there is the figure of a human hand with the index finger extended and pointing toward the heavens. A kindly townsman told me that more than two generations ago the congregation was ministered to by a venerable old pastor whose favorite gesture in the pulpit was the upraised hand and the extended forefinger, always pointing in the direction of the Infinite. When he died, the congregation, in seeking to honor his memory, arranged to have the figure of his hand set atop the steeple. Through all the years since it has continued his ministry in effective and eloquent silence, symbolic of the "upward call of God."

On second thought, however, that is precisely what every

church steeple does. It calls men to lift their thoughts upward toward high and holy things. Every cripple selling lead pencils from the sidewalk is a challenge to the rest of us to lift our hearts in thanksgiving to God for healthy bodies and strong limbs. The trust placed in us by a little child (and who among us is not some small child's hero) is a sight draft payable only in terms of our finest efforts and purest purposes.

There is a highly important word in the question "Where do you think you are going?" which we are apt to overlook. It is so easy to *think* we are going in one direction when, actually, we are speeding in another. There was the commuter, for instance, who boarded a Chicago elevated train *thinking* it was headed for Evanston, and who did not discover his mistake until he happened to glance out the window of the coach and see the south-side "Jackson Park" on a station platform. *Thinking* had not changed the direction of the train, no matter how honest or sincere he had been in his thinking. The Negro spiritual, "All God's Chillun Got Wings," voices a timely warning in a plaintive melody when it sings, "Ev'rybody talkin' 'bout heab'n ain't goin' dere."

Any of us will be wise if we take a little time off from the wild scramble we call "the struggle for existence" to ask ourselves a simple and searching question. "Suppose I arrive at the point toward which I am driving so furiously, will I then be where I want to be?" In the event that we are elected, that the business deal turns out as we have planned, that we move into the new house, that we marry the money or are pledged to the fraternity, will that mean that we have really found the thing we are searching for? Or, to put it in concrete terms, will we achieve security by becoming economically secure, will we find real peace by achieving peace of mind, will we experience actual happiness in the process of buying something or have the abundant life just because we have accumulated an abundance of things?

The worst fooled person is that one who fools himself. He is so sure that the one who fools him is right.

In the meantime the upward call of God is sounding in our ears in every great hymn we sing, in the pages of our New Testament which accuse us, in every cry of need that resounds within our conscience, and in every holy cause that seeks to enlist us in a crusade for righteousness.

We face the constant danger of going in a direction entirely opposite that one in which God is going.

Where do you *think* you're going?

Where *are* you going?

7

so what?

A HIGHLY loquacious individual had been holding forth at great length on an inconsequential theme in an evident attempt to impress a group of idlers with his knowledge of the subject. Using technical terms which he did not attempt to define and with a torrent of words designed to awe his hearers without enlightening them, he finally arrived at a conclusion by crossing a very shaky bridge. Whereupon a bright-eyed youth at the edge of the crowd who had been quick to detect the pretense, called out, "So what?"

The young man's slang is a popular expression usually used to pierce bubbles and reduce pretenses to their proper size. Actually, however, it is a demand for the essential truth in a situation—for a courageous facing of the facts.

In our Sunday-school days we heard the story of Absalom, the conceited and reckless son of King David, who arose in revolt against his aged father and was killed in a battle that determined the future of the kingdom. The old king, doting to the last, was waiting at the palace gate hoping for some good word, when a runner was seen coming over the horizon. The messenger's news was all about the outcome of the battle and the success of the king's arms. To this David listened more or less patiently. Then with infinite pathos in his voice he put the question that was really of interest to him, "Is it

78

well with the young man Absalom?" Everything else—victory, personal pride, even the welfare of the kingdom—faded into relative insignificance in comparison with the fate of the headstrong boy.

A very large share of the news of the day, radio opinion, common conversation, and public discussion, deals with issues that are quite superficial. Much of it, in addition, is what the psychologists call "rationalization"; a part of it is nothing better than a noisy effort to evade the facts; still another part is a deliberate attempt to make the truth appear to be something it is not. A generation reared in the midst of such sophistry and messy thinking owes it to itself to pause occasionally and ask itself, quite seriously, "So what?"

Let us tear away all hypocrisy and ask ourselves a few intimate questions with relentless honesty. Are we compelling life to serve us well, or are we accepting pretenses and substitutes for life at its best?

I. What Are We Actually Aiming At?

We may find this question a bit difficult to answer because we have been deluding ourselves into thinking we were living for high and noble purposes, whereas in truth we have been serving causes that are mean and contemptible. By giving selfishness a glamorous name, we have persuaded ourselves that we were actually unselfish.

A particularly bald and unvarnished illustration of this rather common offense against integrity is the case of the individual who, finding himself without employment, suddenly develops a passionate interest in some "cause," enlists the support of others, perfects an organization, and contrives to have himself elected an executive secretary with a salary and an expense account. The religious field, and particularly that of temperance reform, has offered a happy hunting ground for this type of individual with the result that the cause of religion has been cursed with a plethora of competing organizations.

It is so easy for a vigorous individual with deep convictions to persuade himself that he is offering himself as a sacrifice when he is really offering himself at a good price.

It is not that such persons are deliberate hypocrites. Far from it. The probabilities are that no more than a very small percentage of them are in any way insincere. It is only that their motives are badly mixed and that they are actually unable to distinguish between the true and the untrue, the generous and the selfish.

In no field of religious activities are motives more seriously mixed than in the matter of giving. It is always a temptation to measure our benevolence by that of others—to give as much as "they" do to save our pride, or to head the list for the sake of the prestige that goes with generosity. Occasionally—perhaps only rarely—we encounter one who gives largely that he may thereafter dictate the policies, but such giving always damns instead of blessing.

Jesus insisted that we should pray for those who "despitefully use us," and he could have added, with some appropriateness, "and those who outdo us." He who has learned to pray for his rival, in complete sincerity, has attained a rare degree of spiritual maturity.

He will be exercising a wise spiritual precaution who, having offered an elaborate excuse for not doing his plain duty, or having taken grievous offense because his idea was not accepted, or having been sadly disappointed because he was not made chairman of the committee, sits down with the facts and asks himself the question, "So what?" If the cause of Christ is his actual concern, few such things will ever discourage him for long.

II. Are You Trying to Make the Rules?

Harold B. Walker, in a fascinating book entitled *Power to Manage Yourself,* tells the story of a hillbilly who made a great reputation for himself as a marksman. Other woodsmen who followed him found rings marked in chalk on trees, stumps, fences, and gates. In the exact center of each there was a bullet hole. Someone asked him one day to explain the secret of his skill. "That's easy," he said. "I just shoot the hole and then go draw the ring around it."

They are legion who, like the hillbilly, undertake to make the rules of life to suit themselves. When they have sinned, they do not repent. Instead, they invent a code of conduct that justifies their sinning, and thereafter live as though that rule were the divine law of life.

There are those, for instance, who find Jesus' judgment on the subject of divorce uncomfortable, and thereafter they dismiss it quite airily as being "impractical for this modern generation." If his counsel concerning the other cheek or the second mile is not entirely convenient, it is brushed aside with the comment that it "will not work in a world like ours." If his principles, when applied to the problem of race relations, call for an entirely new and upgraded attitude, it is pointed out that "he did not live under the social pressures with which we have to contend." If the ethics of Jesus flatly contradict their economic conduct, they are apt to say, "But a man has to live, doesn't he?"

One of the first lessons the young child is expected to learn is the simple proposition that he lives in a world for which he does not make the rules. The most painful experience through which he ever passes is apt to be his first day in school when, after having lived for six years in a world where he has ruled as a totalitarian, he finds himself on the grounds of a school and under the authority of a democratic society. In the succeeding years his maturing can be measured by the skill with which he adjusts himself to the world in which he is compelled to live.

That person's education is well advanced who has learned that he does not make the laws of life—that they are made for him, and that his happiness and spiritual destiny depend upon his ability to live inside the law.

No chemist, upon entering his laboratory, ever presumes to dictate the laws which are to govern the atoms and the molecules during the processes of his research. No engineer undertakes to write the rules that maintain order in the area of his particular science. Instead, each sets out on a determined search to discover the laws that are already established, knowing only that as he conforms can he hope for success. If this principle of procedure prevails everywhere else in our universe, is it conceivable that it can be set aside in the field of morals or that of the human spirit?

It is a basic conviction of that one who is truly Christian that the will of God concerning morals and the human spirit has been revealed to man in the life and person of Jesus Christ. As "the way, the truth, and the life," he is our final authority. His moral judgments and his spiritual decisions can no more be set aside than can the law of gravity or that of chemical cohesion. Any person who shoots holes and then draws rings about them may satisfy his conceits by so doing, but he does not satisfy the inexorable moral and spiritual demands of God. It will never be well with such an Absalom.

III. Are We Really Free to Choose?

One of our most common delusions, and the one with which we are most commonly compelled to contend, is our almost pathetic confidence in our own freedom. We recite with much glibness the scripture which assures us that we shall "know the truth," and that it will "make us free." Unfortunately, however, insofar as many areas of our lives are concerned, we are afraid to know the truth lest it prove uncomfortable or demanding. As some wag once remarked, "Ye shall know the truth and the truth shall make you mad."

We Americans boast much of our "four freedoms," and it is true that they are the greatest blessings modern men know. They have been bequeathed to us by heroic fathers who probably thought more profoundly upon the subject of government than did any generation that ever lived. Political orators extol our freedoms with a passion that is both commendable and justified, and the Voice of America is undertaking to convince the world, and especially the millions of the world's population behind curtains of various densities, that democracy guarantees freedom to all men. But Christian candor compels us to ask ourselves just how free we really are.

How free have we been, for example, to make up our minds concerning political matters? To what extent has the pressure of our labor union, employer's association, or our economic associates determined our thinking and made our choices for us? How far has our political affiliation predetermined our judgments? Have we actually sought to know the truth with any seriousness or open-mindedness?

Suppose we consider for a moment, purely for illustrative purposes, the question of our independent and free thinking concerning the Bible. The discovery of the Dead Sea Scrolls, with the astounding new light they throw on the whole question of the first-century Christian church, bids fair to revolutionize scholarly opinion in a score of crucial fields of biblical research. At the moment there seems to be some credible evidence indicating that Jesus of Nazareth may have been profoundly influenced in his social and religious thinking by a strange sect called the Essenes. Until the scrolls were brought to light, relatively little was known about the theology or the social practices of that cult. Now they are coming to life as an amazing society with many of the characteristics which have long been supposed to have originated with Christianity. Sober historians are beginning to hint that Jesus himself may have adopted some of their unique ideas. The implications are revolutionary in the extreme.

Just how far are we free to accommodate our thinking to all this new evidence, and how prone will we be to accept it or denounce it on the basis of its "modernism" or "fundamentalism"? How far will our prejudices and preconceptions permit us to follow the facts in a strictly honest and scientific fashion?

Let us not blame "the times," "sinister influences," "Wall Street," or "our overlords" for the fact that we are not free. The vast majority of our enslavements are the result of our own commitments—our personal surrenders, if you please. The apostle Paul, in writing to the Christians of Rome, said, "Do you not know that if you yield yourselves to anyone as obedient slaves, you are slaves of the one you obey?" (6:16.) In that respect the American Legion, Rotary International, the National Association of Manufacturers, A.F.L., C.I.O., D.A.R., the American Medical Association, Walter Lippmann, and Westbrook Pegler count their "slaves" by the millions. The vast majority of us "belong" to something— political, social, economic, or theological—in almost every sense of that word.

As an illustration of this type of "slavery" there is the case of an editor of a small paper dedicated to a strict theological viewpoint who published an extended editorial attacking the Revised Standard Version of the Bible when it first appeared. Thousands of his readers, trusting him, accepted his judgment without questioning it. When queried in the matter, however, he was compelled to admit that he did not own a copy of the "new Bible," had not seen a copy of it at the time of writing his editorial, and had trusted entirely to the critical opinion of another editor.

At the close of a sermon in the course of which I had felt compelled to speak frankly, as a Christian, concerning certain social conditions in our community, I was approached by one of my official laymen who warned me, "You had better be careful about what you say about such matters. Most of us are Republicans, you know."

When I inquired as to whether or not I had said anything that contradicted the judgment of Jesus, he replied, "I don't know about that, but I do know what the morning paper will say." As if the party platform and the morning paper could be allowed to dictate to the consciences of Christians!

Repeatedly in his letters to the first-century Christians, Paul described himself as a "slave of Jesus Christ." The risen Lord was his undisputed Master. He might be a Hebrew and proud of his race, and he might also be a Pharisee and proud of his faithfulness as such. But if, in order to be unalterably true to his Master, he found it necessary to break with Judaism, he was ready to do so. He was a loyal Jew and a faithful Pharisee only as long as he might be such without violating his vows to the one who had called him out of the blinding light along the Damascus Way. Those were not idle words he used in describing a frightful list of sufferings, persecutions, and terrors; and when he said, "None of these things move me," he was speaking the truth. No one in all the records of religion was ever a more perfectly "integrated personality." At the same time he was probably the most nearly free person who ever lived.

In the light of all the enslavements to which we are subject, we shall do well if we ask ourselves, very strictly, "How free are we?"

Is it well with all these modern Absaloms?

IV. Do We Really Believe in God?

There was something cynical, and also typical, in the war song with the words, "Praise the Lord and pass the ammunition." It is characteristic of modern men to pay God polite compliments and then put their actual trust in the gods of this world—such as ammunition.

A young businessman, hard pressed and sorely tempted, put the whole case into crisp terms when he said, "I believe there is a God, all right. No one can look even a little way under the surface of this world and not be convinced that it was created by some divine Power. But I am also pretty sure that, if I am going to get the things I want out of this life, I am going to have to depend upon myself." And a young woman, also hard pressed but with a slightly more polite manner of expression, said, "I suppose God will help, but I'm afraid he will not help me in time. I've got to do something by tomorrow noon."

Blatant atheists are extremely rare among us. Agnostics who say, "I do not say there is no God; I only say I don't know," are much more numerous. But they are legion who, avowing a confidence that there is such a being as God, proceed to live as though there were none.

There is the Christian businessman who says, "I hate to do it. I feel like a heel. It violates all my Christian conscience and profession, but I have to do it if I am going to stay in business." And there is also the Christian preacher who, even though he is sure he knows the mind of God, avoids speaking truth to the powerful in his congregation because they are powerful.

Perhaps even more to the point is the case of that minister who announced from his pulpit one Sunday morning that he was "worried to death about the mortgage." The following morning a businessman who had been going through deep waters for more than a year telephoned the clergyman to say, "You shook the earth under my feet with that sermon yesterday. For almost a year you have been assuring me that God would see me through my difficulties. Now you confess that you are 'worried to death' about the church debt. That leaves me wondering. If you can't trust God to help with the mortgage on his own house, how can you make me believe he will help me with the mortgage on mine? Isn't he as much interested in the church as he is in my insurance business?"

All too long we have been satisfied with an unemployed faith. We say we have been intellectually confident that God exists, but we have stumbled through life beset by the fear that the evils and the perplexities of this world are too much for him. Real faith is something very much more virile and creative than a mere opinion, no matter how well that opinion may be bulwarked by reason and facts. It is a readiness to walk out on our opinions, trusting them as though they might be expected to hold up under any pressure that life may bring to bear upon them.

It was that kind of faith a little group of churchmen in Kansas exercised when the boom collapsed in their town, leaving seven of them as the sole surviving income producers in the church and with a mortgage coming due within the next six months. Gathered in their beloved sanctuary and determined to pray through to an assurance, they continued on their knees in constant prayer for something more than an hour. Finally one of them announced that he thought he had an intimation of the "leading of the Spirit." At that they all arose, took their seats, and listened intently while he outlined his plan.

"We cannot expect God to do anything for us until we have ourselves gone the full limit of our ability to help ourselves. I am therefore proposing that each of us lay the last penny in his possession before the Lord. This we will use in meeting our obligations as far as our funds go. When we have reduced ourselves to our last penny, I am confident God will come to our assistance."

In a magnificent adventure of daring faith the other six joined their leader, every man emptying his pockets completely. The total amount of money that lay upon the altar, before the pulpit, amounted to slightly more than $38. With an unwavering faith they voted to use it an effort to lift the debt. Then they "waited on the Lord." Call it a miracle, a coincidence, or any other name you please; but within the space of hours helping hands appeared. Within the space of days funds were available to pay off all the church's indebtedness, and within a year each of those seven was again on his own feet in his own business.

There was something magnificent in the faith of those seven humble country churchmen. They were intellectually convinced of the fact that God was a reality, but their faith was much more than a convincing argument. It was a willingness to act aggressively and positively on the basis of their opinion. And as they acted, they were justified.

The cynic who listens to our protestations of confidence in the doctrine of God, and then observes our lack of willingness to trust God, can be excused perhaps for exclaiming, "So what?"

"I bid every one among you not to think of himself more highly than he ought to think" —Rom. 12:3

8

do you think you own the earth?

BILLY had long been accustomed to go through his days in a high-handed, callous, and ruthless sort of fashion. Because he was a self-made man and a little more than ordinarily successful, he believed strongly in his own superiority and enjoyed posing in a masterful role. Like many another of his kind, however, he was mortally afraid of exhibiting any trace of emotion or sentiment, and took pains to assure his associates that "every man has to look out for himself in a world like this." It was not that he was essentially selfish, or that he was naturally brutal. At heart he was a rather decent sort. But his imperious manner, his brusque speech, and his big voice served constant notice to the world about him that it was to get out of his way. Then one day a rather mild-mannered man on the staff, exasperated to the point of exploding, suddenly demanded of him, *"Do you think you own the earth?"*

It was a natural and understandable outburst from one who had nursed a real grievance through many months, and Billy well deserved the rebuke; but coming as it did from an otherwise patient and soft-spoken individual, it proved to be something of a shock, and he found great difficulty in trying to understand how he had offended anyone.

The Christian church in the city of Rome was made up,

89

with rare exceptions, of nobodies—slaves, the declassed, the riff raff, and the humble. Nowhere outside the Christian fellowship were any of them accorded anything like social status or standing. They could offer their testimonies and be heard with respect; they could voice opinions concerning the affairs of the congregation and be sure their ideas were given proper consideration; they could meditate upon the great facts of faith and know that their fellow Christians would listen when they expressed their ideas. Many of them found it to be something of an intoxicating kind of experience to be somebody for even one little hour in one small kitchen; but, as often happens when the unrecognized get recognition, some of them had become impossible. As a wise administrator (and also as a shrewd psychologist) the apostle Paul wrote them a bit of sound advice: "I bid everyone among you not to think of himself more highly than he ought to think."

I. The Basic Values of Self-Respect

This sermon proposes to make no appeal in behalf of Casper Milquetoast and his apologetic self-effacement. There are few people more irritating than that one who, in a transparent effort to ingratiate himself, assumes a mock pose of vast humility as he apologizes profusely for offenses that he never committed and seeks pardon for affronts that were never noticed. Genuine humility is one of the fairest of all the graces; false modesty is one of the most offensive of all the hypocrisies.

It is one of the distinctions of our scriptures that they invariably represent God as holding man in great respect, in spite of any sinfulness of which he may have been guilty, The book of Genesis, for example, following its recital of the story of man's creation, says, "And God saw everything that he had made, and behold, it was very good" (1:31)—

and that included man! Ezekiel, the prophet, says that when he was summoned to his prophetic work by the Most High, he was thus challenged: "Stand upon your feet, and I will speak with you" (2:1), and the Prophet Micah quotes the Almighty as speaking of man as though he were a highly honorable creature (6:8). There is something very thrilling in the thought that God does not expect man to cringe in his presence. As a matter of fact, the prophet Habakkuk was honored when he dared to challenge the divine administration of justice between nations, and Abraham was called the father of the faithful after he had demanded that "the Judge of all the earth do right" (Gen. 18:25). If the Creator holds us in such high esteem, it follows inevitably that we should esteem ourselves in equally high measure. If we are creatures of the Eternal, born in the image of God, we dare not sin against our own dignity.

A stalwart independence and an inner sense of self-respect are among the chief identifications of the image of God in which we were created. It has been a confidence in this intimacy of comradeship with the Divine which has distinguished the great spiritual and moral leaders of every generation. But it is not the great nor the famous who, alone of all mankind, have been born free to do their own thinking. Intellectual and moral independence are a part of the birthright of every man whatever be his race, color, or inheritance.

An old Texas Negro, standing beside his team of mules at the end of the row of cotton, was being solicited to make a contribution to a small Negro college by the president of the institution and by the white man who accompanied him. The white-haired old farmer appeared to be deeply impressed by the fact that two such dignitaries should take the trouble to cross a plowed field in the heat of the day to talk to him about such a matter.

The white man had presented the case with much tact,

and the black man had listened attentively. At last, when the time came for him to make some reply, he took off his dusty old felt hat, scratched his head meditatively for a moment, and then said, "Doctor, I surely appreciate it that you have taken the trouble to come out here on a hot day to talk to a poor old man like me. And I'm going to give you something. I don't know how much, but I'm going to give you some money. You see, I've got to think this whole thing over."

Then, hesitating a moment, he went on in a slightly different tone. "You see, doctor, I ain't never been in no college in all my life. I never had no chance to go to any school when I was little, and I ain't never seen inside a college. I don't know what one is like. That's just the reason why I've always had to do all my own thinking."

That afternoon, at the end of a row of cotton, a humble man all unwittingly took his stand on the basis of the image of God in which he was created!

In spite of the tide of cynicism with which modern society is inundated, it must be said that man has a long list of reasons for holding himself in high respect. As Fred Hoyle, the English astronomer, has said in his *Frontiers of Astronomy:*

Man's claim to have progressed far beyond his fellow animals must be supported, not by his search for food, warmth, and shelter (however ingeniously conducted) but by his penetration into the very fabric of the Universe. It is in this world of ideas and in the relation of his brain to the Universe itself, that the superiority of Man lies. The rise of Man may justly be described as an adventure in Ideas.[1]

A scientist with a profound Christian faith put the matter in dramatic fashion in one of his classroom lectures one day

[1] (New York: Harper & Bros., 1955), p. 1.

when he described God as being greatly excited while he watched a researcher in his laboratory pursuing an elusive principle which he hoped would explain a set of facts. Standing erect and impersonating the Creator in a moment of great enthusiasm, he fairly shouted, "I believe he's going to get it. He's almost got it!! He has it!!! Hooray!" Perhaps he was a bit "anthropomorphic," as the theologians would say. That is, perhaps he did impute human motives to the Divine. But a thoughtful senior said, "I believe God is just like that."

Man's upward climb has been a tedious one and, at times, beset with almost unbelievable difficulty. But *it has been upward!* There have been glorious hours in every century, and there have been great souls in every generation. The lessons man has learned and the knowledge he has accumulated en route combine to make an almost incredible total. It is said that if any one student should set out to take all the courses offered by the graduate school at Harvard University alone, it would keep him enrolled for the next three hundred years.

The problems with which this generation is bedeviled are legion and also of infinite complexity. Every riddle we have solved has laid bare a dozen others, more difficult, that await solution. The inventions we have devised in the hope of making life luxurious have made it tense and sometimes tempestuous. There are those doubting and timorous souls who declare that man cannot long continue to bear the burden of civilization—that his spirit is not equal to the strain—but even our secular and materialistic generation has produced a Schweitzer, a Kagawa, a Laubach, and a Toynbee. In invoicing the capacities of the spirit of the common man, we have not yet even scratched the surface. From the walks of the commonest among us there continues to come a succession of stirring tales of heroism, nobility, and idealism.

Let it be said with all boldness: we have a divine right to self-respect.

II. The Hazards of Conceit

It imposes no great strain upon one's imagination to conjure up a scene which doubtless occurred many times inside the early Christian congregations when some new convert, in the first burst of his enthusiasm following the inflow of the Holy Spirit upon his life, undertook to instruct his fellow Christians in the deep things of the soul. The profound sense of joy and peace which possessed him was so powerful and so transforming that he found it difficult to believe any other believer had ever experienced anything like it. As a consequence, he became something of a problem. His conceit, however innocently conceived, had the effect of disrupting the fellowship. He was so sure of his own salvation, so confident in his own testimony, and so insistent that other men's experience should conform to his own pattern. The apostle Paul, having seen hundreds, perhaps thousands, come into the light of life in Christ, knew full well that no two persons ever have exactly the same experience or ever react in precisely the same way. In warning the Roman Christians against all forms of spiritual conceit, he said, "Let no man think more highly of himself than he ought to think."

There is a versatility about the Holy Spirit that is almost infinite. Inside the heart of one penitent he works a work of great joy; inside the heart of another his presence is attended by a great sense of calm; and within the heart of still another he may produce a tumult of emotions.

An aged theological professor who had had an amazingly varied experience with young men who were trying to work their way through to a logically defensible position in the Christian faith, once suggested that a meeting of the three blind men whom Jesus had healed might have been an interesting affair. The first one, aglow with excitement as a result of his new-found vision, would probably have described his healing with a single rapturous sentence: "He touched my eyes and I saw!" But one of the others, quite confident that it could not possibly be as simple as that, would have remonstrated, saying, "Unless he touched you twice and repeated the ritual, as he did in my case, you do not really see. I beg of you, pray for the second divine work of grace. It is wonderful." The third, meanwhile, quite sure of himself and feeling superior to the other two, might have said, "Brethren, I am sure that you are very sincere and that doubtless you have some measure of light, but I am also very sure that yours is only a partial vision. In fact you never will really see until you go down as I did to the Pool of Siloam and there wash the clay from your eyes. It's the washing that does it!" And yet all three of the blind men were seeing, thanks to the versatility of the grace of God— seeing everything except the fact that their fellows also saw clearly.

There is nothing more unchristian in a Christian than the spiritual conceit which encourages a forgiven man to set himself above his brethren. Therefore, let no man among us think more highly of his Christian perfection than he ought to think!

Next in seriousness to our spiritual conceits are our social conceits. So many lines divide us—economic, social, political, linguistic, cultural, religious. Jesus was undertaking to erase some of them when he said, "He that is not against us is for us" (Mark 9:40). S. Parkes Cadman, the fascinating pulpiteer of a generation ago, was accustomed to say, "When you build your denominational walls high to shut yourselves in, you will render yourselves a great service if you will climb to their top occasionally to see how many wonderful people you have shut out." The modern controversialists who labor to keep the church of Jesus Christ divided against itself are among the most serious sinners of this generation because they think of themselves and their own opinions more highly than they ought to think.

The American people generally are grievous sinners in this regard. We are so proud of our achievements, our resources, and our abundance, as though they were all the result of our superior ability, industry, or intelligence. It comes as a profound shock to the average American tourist when he discovers people of other lands who are refined, artistic, and thrifty. Many a young missionary going overseas as a herald of the cross of Christ has been amazed to discover that vast sections of the non-Christian world are highly civilized and that the people enjoy a rich culture and have a religious faith which includes many values. One young woman—an honor graduate from a famous American university—confided in a traveling companion in an ancient library in China, "I have a strange feeling—as though I were only a little better than a barbarian."

The dean of the graduate school of one of America's finest universities, and the head of the philosophy department of the same school, were spending a year in China prior to the war in an effort to assist that government in setting up its national university system. Among the members of the commission with which they were working were several brilliant young Chinese scholars who had been, in previous years, enrolled in some of their courses in the American school.

One of these young scholars, as a gesture of great friendliness, invited the American professors to accompany him one evening for the purpose of seeing some famous Chinese actors present an ancient classical play. It was a gala occasion, which would have corresponded on a cultural level with a first-night affair of the Metropolitan Opera. Not long after the little party of two professors and three Chinese scholars had been seated in the playhouse, some richly gowned Chinese were noticed moving to other seats some distance away. Within a short space of time the Americans found themselves in splendid isolation, with no other company than that of their Chinese scholar-friends. One of the young men, very reluctant to tell them the truth, finally confessed under pressure that "westerners use such large amounts of dairy products in their daily diet that it results in a body odor that is quite offensive to a cultured Oriental."

Under such circumstances perhaps our text should read, "Let no man think of himself more highly than he ought to think, for to others he may stink!" In reckoning up our national, as well as our personal, liabilities, we need ample space for our conceits.

III. How Do Our Conceits Look to God?

Serious as the question of our conceits may be as we attempt to live among our neighbors—national as well as personal—in this modern world, we shall be inviting disaster if we do not ask ourselves in a spirit of great humility, "How do our conceits look to God?"

Suppose, for example, that we ask ourselves an extremely simple as well as an extremely complicated question: "How much of our money did we make by our own efforts?"

Many years ago a young man, almost helplessly crippled as a result of polio, became convinced that a fortune could be made by buying corner lots in the city of Minneapolis. Using a few thousand dollars he had contrived to save by dint of painful economy, he made down payments on half a dozen. Then he sat in his wheel chair and watched the people pass. As the crowds became more and more dense, the value of his lots rose because business follows the crowds. Pursuing his policy through a period of fifty years, he accumulated a fortune of nearly $3,000,000 which he bequeathed for the establishment of a crippled children's hospital. "The people made my fortune for me," he said at the age of eighty-five, "by walking past my corner lots."

Mark, in composing his Gospel, gave us a highly suggestive phrase when he said, "The earth produces of itself" (4:28). And to that a physician added the admission, "the body heals itself."

The ancient Hebrews were very wise and observing when they introduced into their ritual, well toward its beginning, the psalmist's exalted word, "The earth is the Lord's and the fulness thereof," and then ordained that all men should tithe the increase of their flocks and the yield of their fields as an evidence of their reverence for Jehovah.

The inculcation of the spirit of reverence in the case of our fathers was a relatively easy matter, for they lived close to the good earth. If they drank of a clear flowing stream, they were reminded of the good God who gave them refreshments. If they sat about their blazing fires through the long winter evenings, their cellars full of home-canned food and their barns full of grain and cattle, they were quite naturally inspired to give thanks to the God of the land. But there is very little about a water faucet to remind a modern man of his Maker. He is much more apt to think of the unpaid plumber. And where is the modern family that sits about a steam radiator or enjoys radiant heating and offers a prayer of gratitude to God?

Modern men suffer from no more deadly maladies than those which result from a lack of reverence. The scriptures inquire quite relentlessly, "Which of you by being anxious can add one cubit to his span of life?" (Matt. 6:27), and warn us with the words, "Never be conceited" (Rom. 12:16).

Suppose, for example, that God should go off on a holiday

some Sunday morning, saying, "It's the only day I can ever get off from my work."

What would happen to all the steel bridges in the world, the electrically operated machines, the gasoline-driven automobiles, the synthetic drugs that are being administered in our hospitals, or the planes that fly through the stratosphere? What, in a word, would become of all man's conceits?

The Athenians who gathered on Mars Hill to hear the apostle Paul were accustomed to spend their time hearing and talking about new things, and they were distinctly disappointed in the "babbler" who discussed the vast theme of the Resurrection, so much so that they dismissed him rather condescendingly after a little while and sauntered off after some new preacher. But they stand judged today as intellectually and spiritually incompetent because they had no capacity to understand the majesty of the thing Paul said when he declared, "In him [God] we live and move and have our being" (Acts 17:28). No more profound word was ever spoken from that famous forum.

A flyer a mile above Manhattan Island finds it quite impossible to distinguish the figures of the hurrying throngs on Wall Street. Three miles up he can scarcely identify the Empire State Building which is the tallest structure ever raised by the hands of man. According to one aviation engineer, it would be impossible for the pilot to pick out the speck that is New York if he were fifty miles aloft. How small our biggest must look to God! How slow and stupid we must seem to be at times to the Divine; how oblivious we are to the obvious and how blind we are to the truth! How slow to learn from our experiences!

No man really grows as a soul who has within him no sense of wonder, no spirit of reverence, no capacity to stand in awe. No life can possibly be rewarding to one who had been made in the image of God if the liver of that life is insensible to the upward call of God. Day in and day out, every hour of the day, we are being summoned to the heights, and always the "deep is calling to the deep" and is not being heard.

"I bid everyone among you, therefore, not to think of himself more highly than he ought to think."

We do not own the earth; we are only tenants in a world where someone else has fixed the rules!

*"The measure you give
will be the measure you get"*
—Mark 4:24

9

don't kid yourself!

A GROUP of idlers gathered outside the barber shop in a little country town was engaged in a general argument. Everybody had an opinion, and each one was ready to defend his personal judgment against all comers. It was actually a free-for-all, but two rather undersized individuals at the center of the huddle seemed to be the principal contenders. One of them had evidently made a statement the other could not countenance, for he cried out in a voice that betokened supreme contempt, "Don't kid yourself!" And with that he strode away in high dudgeon.

Modern life has grown to be very bewildering. For those of us who have passed the meridian and who learned to do our living in the prewar world, it is especially baffling. Plastics, jet-propelled transportation, government by decree rather than by law, synthetics, television, twenty million Americans engaged in world travel at government expense, existentialism, the Barthian theology, psychosomatic medicine, nuclear fission, the rise of Russia to the status of a world power, microfilming, psychotherapy—these and an almost interminable list of other new life-factors have had the effect of uprooting human society and setting mankind off to an entirely new way of living.

The most sinister aspect of the situation appears in the fact that vast multitudes have lost all confidence in moral principles and assume that the difference between right and wrong makes no difference. The assembly line has had the effect of robbing men of their pride in their handiwork; mass hysteria has had the effect of robbing men of their independent moral judgment; spiritual illiteracy has had the effect of benumbing the public conscience on the subject of "righteousness, temperance, and judgment to come."

We are becoming fatalists without knowing the meaning of the term. There is a widespread assumption, especially among our youth, that nothing a person does makes much difference. True, there are some things advantageous and some other things disadvantageous, some things profitable and some things unprofitable, but to a generation that seldom gives a thought to the fact that we are born to live in two worlds—this one and the next—morals lose their significance, and spirituality is dismissed as pure sentimentality, if not cheap emotionalism. All this is of the essence of the communistic philosophy which insists that we live under a totalitarianism of economics.

In recent years there has developed a vast confidence in psychology. Our fathers' generation, convicted of sin, cried out, "What must I do to be saved?" Our sons crowd the reception rooms of the psychiatric clinics, hoping to be furnished with a technique that will relieve them from their frustrations, inhibitions, and complexes. Men are not being warned that they are sinners; instead, they are being assured that they are victims—victims of systems, conditioning, environment, glandular secretions or anything else to which can be assigned the role of scapegoat.

The fruitage is inevitable and should not be a surprise to anyone: juvenile delinquency, a dismaying divorce rate, widespread alcoholism, political and social corruption, industrial violence, an intolerable burden of taxation due to the increased costs of a regulatory and protective government, and a long list of cancerous growths on our urbanized civilization. There is a desperate need for some compelling voice to cry out to this generation of sophisticated moderns, saying, "Don't kid yourself! You are living in a world that is subject to law, and in such a world the lawbreaker is doomed."

I. Ours Is an Orderly World

Arthur H. Compton, one of the great scientists of all time, said some years ago that the greatest scientific discovery thus far made is that ours is an orderly world, subject in every detail to the government of law. There are no outlaw spaces anywhere in the universe. There is no area of life that is not subject to a system of laws especially and precisely designed for the maintenance of an invariable order. This principle rules out any possibility of accident or chance and ushers in an entirely new and revolutionary concept of life.

There was a time, for example, when men thought that chemistry and medicine were fields in which whimsy was in control. Those were the days of incantations, magic, ritualism, and sacrifice. Disease was believed to be a form of punishment meted out by whatever gods there were, on the basis of any impulse that might be at the moment in control of the gods' minds. Drought and disaster were the direct results of man's failure properly to placate or flatter little local divinities who were always jealous without reason. Great cataclysms were displays of divine wrath in the face of which humanity was helpless and hopeless because it was defenseless.

Then came the day when someone discovered a law. A drug administered under certain controlled conditions produced certain definite results. Whenever the conditions were repeated, the results recurred. Then came the realization that a dependable principle was operating; something made the results predictable and reliable. Once that a man knew the law which governed the facts, he was in a position to control those facts up to the limit of that law. This discovery revealed man's ability in some measure to control the world in which he lived. He was no longer at the mercy of whimsy; he was in a position to create the whimsy he preferred.

Working his way through the implications of this principle, Louis Pasteur developed his theory of the microbic origin of disease. When he had established the fact that one disease was the result of the multiplication of bacilli within the human blood stream, he was in a position to begin the search for the bacillus which caused another malady, and then another, and another. Then as a logical development of the theory, there followed a series of inoculations and anti-toxins designed to create artificial immunities. There was no magic about it, no ritual or ceremony, no incantations or burning sacrifices. Instead there was much burning of the midnight oil and an undeviating obedience to whatever laws were known to govern the bacteria. No true scientist ever dreams of trying to outwit or defy the law, and neither does he attempt to achieve results without making every possible effort to inform himself concerning the working of the laws. Any such anarchical procedure would be a frontal attack upon himself, as a scientist, and a repudiation of his entire scientific philosophy.

What the physical scientist has done for the world of things, Jesus did for the things of the spirit. As Galileo discovered and described the law of the pendulum, or as Pasteur laid bare the ways of microbes, so Jesus made plain the principles by which the human spirit lives and co-operates with the Divine Spirit.

When Jesus said, for example, that the meek are the fortunate people, for they are to inherit the earth, he was setting forth a plain statement of an invariable law of life. When he laid it down as a fixed principle that the pure in heart were the only ones who may see God, he was acting in no arbitrary manner. Instead, he was proceeding as a modern scientist does when he explains an invariable law. The chemist who describes the process by which we can have hydrochloric acid is in no sense of the word dictatorial. He is only exercising his proper function as a guide in the field of chemistry. Both the chemist and Jesus are rendering us services of great import when they make plain the conditions in their respective areas under which we may expect to have life at its best.

Imagine, if you can, what might happen if a sophisticated youth, utterly without experience, invaded the laboratory in which an experienced scientist was working with chemical solutions, test tubes, retorts, and other delicate apparatus. Suppose he began tossing explosives about with reckless abandon and laughing the chemist to scorn when he warned of the direful possible results. Think, if you can, of the youth saying, "I am an emancipated liberal, a free soul, and an independent thinker who despises conventions. I propose to play with these explosives as I please. I have no interest in laws; I want life, and I intend to have it. I'll make my own laws!"

The chemist would probably say, providing he could hold his patience, "You may be very smart, and you are probably a clever youngster, but no one ever hoodwinks the atoms or bullies the molecules. They perform according to a system of laws with which no man has ever been able to interfere. Understand and invoke those laws and they will serve you well; ignore or defy their ways of working and they will destroy you."

If the chemist were to use the youth's own vocabulary, he would say, "Don't kid yourself!"

II. The Measure You Get

Let us be completely honest about the matter. All of us are trying to get something out of life. There are those philosophers and psychologists who insist that there is no such thing as unselfishness—that each of us does what he does for some selfish reason—for the sake of satisfying some inner urge. Even the bestowal of charity or the rendering of service, they say, is an effort to find some inner satisfaction for ourselves. Perhaps by stretching the definition of our terms, such a case can be made out; but whatever the name we give it, all our efforts are made to satisfy one or more of the four dominant desires of life.

The psychologists, having analyzed all the human motives scientifically, declare there are but four and that by these all men are moved: (a) the desire to be loved; (b) the desire to belong to something; (c) the desire to own something; and (d) the desire to create something. Everything we try to get out of life is related in some way to at least one of these four.

Call it happiness, success, economic security, peace of mind, honor, or what you will, every man spends life—sometimes prodigally—in an effort to satisfy some inner hunger. The two most common questions we hear are: "What do I get out of it?" and "What is the payoff?" Inexorable forces drive us; inner thirsts and hungers we are sometimes unable to understand continue to lash us to the task of living and will not let us rest. There is an irresistible desire to get.

If we put our basic scientific principle to work on the problem, we shall be driven directly to the proposition that some law governs our getting. If we can discover it, we shall then find ourselves in charge of our life income. And if we turn to our New Testament, we shall discover that Jesus cited the law in its simplest terms: "The measure you give will be the measure you get."

III. The Measure You Give

Two soldier boys in the Pullman were discussing some matter of intense interest to lads away from home and for the first time in their lives subject to strict discipline. After they had gone on for some time in animated conversation, one of them exclaimed with evident disgust, "Life is a funny game, ain't it?" to which the other replied, "I never thought it was a game; I always figured it was a gamble."

But life is neither a game nor a gamble. It is a delicately balanced affair that operates on a strictly scientific principle—*we get as we give!*

There are those scholars who think that the saying may have been a popular proverb of the times, and that Jesus was only quoting it. The authors of the New Testament never used quotation marks to show that some of their material was copied. It is possible that the proverb was a popular saying with which Jesus' hearers were quite familiar, but at any rate Jesus placed his stamp of approval on it and laid it down as a basic principle of life. We can accept it as his statement of the law. The important thing to know is not whether it was an original saying or something borrowed, but whether or not it is true and dependable. Jesus said it was. That settles it for a Christian, and ought to settle it for all other men as well. But, in addition, the principle of getting by giving has behind it the authentication of centuries of experience.

According to the psychologists' analysis the first dominant desire of life is our longing for love—for the feeling that we are important, that in the life of someone we are supremely necessary. They further tell us that one of the causes of juvenile delinquency is a widespread fear among youngsters

107

that they are "not wanted," that because of broken homes they have developed emotional insecurity, or that because of the tensions of modern life they have become imbued with the idea that they have achieved importance if they have succeeded in getting their names into the newspapers or on police blotters. Among adults a corresponding perversion of the desire to be loved expresses itself in a variety of social misdemeanors. There are those, for example, who rush into print, or into police courts, with frantic confessions of crimes of which they are not actually guilty, hoping thereby to get public attention for a fleeting hour. Free from the fear of conviction, they are able to bask in the knowledge that their names are appearing in boldfaced type, even as liars.

Every moral or spiritual perversion consists of the misuse of some legitimate interest, emotion, or activity. The desire to be loved, basic as it is in every human life, may become a blessing or a curse, depending upon the skill with which we manage it and the faithfulness with which we obey the laws according to which it performs. Nowhere does Jesus' principle—you get as you give—prove itself more readily or more completely than when we undertake to win the love of the world by loving the world, to earn the respect of our fellows by respecting them, to be esteemed important by making ourselves important, to feel necessary by making ourselves necessary to someone or to some cause.

The unlovely are always unloved, those who do not hold themselves in high respect are certain to suffer from the contempt of their neighbors, those who go out in the morning looking for trouble will come home before nightfall with their hands full of it.

The solution of the problem of delinquency—whether it is juvenile or adult—will have been found if we can somehow convince those who believe they are unwanted that in Christ they can make themselves highly desirable.

No man ever succeeded in winning another person's love by contending for it. Neither nations nor individuals ever succeeded in buying love; no price has ever been high enough to make the purchase. It is a proven principle of life that we gain love as we give it away. For that reason Jesus said, "Greater love has no man than this, that a man lay down his life for his friends." (John 15:13.)

For the unloved and the unlovely the solution of the problem is simple. Let them forget themselves. Let them cease to stand guard over their rights; let them end their search for honors and bestow honors instead; let them cease looking for love and go about looking for those in need of love. Let them move the center of interest for their lives outside the circumference of their own concerns and settle it inside the circle of other men's needs. Then they will suddenly discover that all of life has taken on an entirely new quality. They are being loved because they love; they are getting because they are giving.

"Don't kid yourself." You cannot live in a vacuum. You will never be loved until you love. It is one of the fundamental laws of life.

The second dominant desire the psychologists have identified is an inner desire to belong—to sense the comradeship of other men devoted to the same cause and dedicated to the same task. The Christian church has incorporated this principle into its creed and taught men to recite, as a part of the ritual, their belief in "the communion of saints."

Some years before the war my travels took me to China. Late one afternoon I was threading through the narrow lanes of the city of Canton with a little party of tourists when the young Chinese who had been guiding us all day dropped back to walk with me. He was a gracious youth, very patient and unusually well spoken, who had done his best to make our visit to his city a great experience.

After he had walked with me for a distance of a few hundred yards, he interrupted his professional conversation to say, "You are a Christian, are you not?" When I replied that I was, and that I was a Christian clergyman, he reached for my hand, grasped it closely, and walked in silence for a little way.

"I hope you do not mind," he said, finally. "I, too, am a Christian. There are not many of us in China, among so many millions, and I sometimes find myself feeling very lonely. But when I clasp hands with you, I feel that I have hold of the church of the living God. It gives me a feeling of great strength." That *was* "the communion of saints."

Deep within the spirit of every normal human being there is an instinctive fear of being alone. We are dealing here with a psychological and a sociological fact of the utmost importance. The sociologists say that man is a gregarious animal; the psychologists say that there is an infectious contagion about a human personality; and the scriptures say that God saw that "it was not good for a man to be alone."

Belonging, however, makes demands at the same time that it bestows benefits, for we get as we give. We belong to a family and have a home; we belong to a city and get police protection; we belong to a nation and get the rights of citizenship. But in each case we are expected to give. To the family we give co-operation and loyalty, to the city we pay taxes, and to the nation we render military service when the occasion demands. Always we gain as we give; our benefits are paid for in terms of faithful service and loyal support.

There is no such thing as complete personal liberty in such a world as ours. The only person who ever lived who could do as he pleased was Robinson Crusoe. But as soon as the shipwrecked adventurer discovered Friday's footprints on the sands of the beach, his liberties were halved. Thereafter there was one spot on which he had no right to build his hut, there was fruit he might not eat, there were duties he had to assume and rights he had to concede. By the coming of the stranger he gained something priceless in the form of companionship, but he paid for his gain in the loss of his liberties. He got as he gave.

It is one of the common experiences of life that we get out of any institution—school, church, or state, to say nothing of the home—exactly in proportion to the way we contribute to it. By giving our friendship, we find we have made friends; by dedicating our lives to our church, we discover that it repays us a hundredfold; by assisting our nation to be clean and strong, we find our rights are guaranteed as well as the glory of our citizenship.

"Don't kid yourself." This world owes you nothing, not even a living, but it offers you a magnificent market wherein you can exchange your finest and best for the best that life holds for any man. You will get as you give; life is ready to bestow great gifts upon you if you in turn are ready to give of your deepest devotion.

Psychologists, sociologists, and economists are agreed concerning the importance of the acquisitive instinct—the basic urge to own something. Our most tragic social disturbances originate in the fact that we either do not understand, or are unwilling to obey, the same law we have been discussing throughout this sermon—that we get as we give.

One of the first words an infant learns to pronounce is the simple and significant word, "mine." When he becomes a man, his stature as a human being—and as a man among men—can be measured by the meaning he attaches to that word. As he comes to the end of his life on this earth, heaven will invoice him in terms of what he has really made his own. He will be estimated by his ideas, dreams, hopes, purposes, and loves—the things that are actually his own, and not by the things he is reputed to possess.

We may have shelves stacked with books, but none of them are our own until they have become a part of us; the walls of our homes may be hung with magnificent art, but it is not actually ours until it has made a difference in us; glorious music may fill the air, but it is not ours until it has filled our hearts.

There is a whimsical little story of a fisherman's daughter who sat beside the sea, knitting. As she went on with her task, she was joined by a fairy prince who offered to assist her. By evening time the two of them had finished a thing of beauty that made the little girl's heart singing glad. Upon waking the next morning, however, she discovered to her dismay that during the night the prince's weaving had all disappeared, and that she had left only that which she had herself woven. In the final accounting, all we own is that which we have made truly our own. Under such circumstances the word "mine" comes to have a very exact meaning.

"Don't kid yourself!" You never really come into possession of anything until you have given, and usually until you have given to the limit.

Never does the image of God in which we were created come closer to the surface than when we feel within us the insistent urge to create—to give expression to the deepest and best of which we are. To be prevented from giving vent to this urge results in what the psychologists call a "frustration"—one of the most serious diseases that ever infects a personality.

There is something very splendid in the "do it yourself" that is just now sweeping the country. It can very easily be justified on the basis of the economies it effects, but the contribution it is making to life for all who share in it is tremendous. The young bank clerk who spends his hours outside the bank in a campaign of applying paint to his cottage has invested something holy in his home—something no amount of money could command. There is something almost divine in the words, "We did it ourselves."

Thus again, in this fourth dominant desire of life—the instinctive urge to create—we witness the working of the law, "You get as you give."

Jesus was indulging in no arbitrary lordship over mankind when he said, "The measure you give will be the measure you get." Rather, he was laying bare a great principle of life and eternal law of living.

Any man who masters the rule in all its infinite implications is well on his way toward the mastery of life. In the light of this law, the slang phrase, "Don't kid yourself," takes on a profound seriousness. It is a humble man's putting of a great law of life.

10

what's the big idea?

Above the roar of the traffic on a heavily traveled boulevard a resounding crash was heard as a light truck plowed into the rear of a big passenger car. Fortunately no one was hurt, but the whole affair was the result of a particularly stupid bit of driving and the damage was considerable. As the driver of the car clambered out to look over the situation, he approached the operator of the truck with fire in his eye and acid in his voice, saying, *"What's the big idea?"*

There come times in the lives of all of us when we are guilty of the crime of stupidity. We have not been actuated by any vicious motive, and our intentions have been in no way immoral. But we have sinned against our neighbors— and more frequently against ourselves—for the simple reason that we did not think. Modern life demands a rather high degree of intelligence, and the law of the land provides serious penalties for those who are guilty of criminal negligence. In a democratic society thoughtlessness, unconcern, and carelessness are capable of becoming actually criminal.

One of America's great industrial concerns publishes an extremely valuable magazine to which has been given the title *Think*. The head of another highly successful organization that employs hundreds of workers sends a letter to all his employees at regular intervals in which he says, in various forms and phrases, "I do not want you to work any harder. I think you are working hard enough. What I really want you to do is to mix more thinking with your working."

When Jesus was asked to identify the first rule of life, he replied with a line that combined two Old Testament texts (Deut. 6:5 and Lev. 19:18), to which he added a word of his own (Matt. 22:37, Mark 12:28-34). Whereas the writer of Deuteronomy had said that a man was to love the Lord with all his heart, and soul, and might, Jesus added, "And with all your mind." The apostle Paul, in a mighty effort to stabilize the life of the Christians of Philippi, wrote them a letter in which he enumerated a long list of great ideas and then very solemnly charged them "to think on these things."

Man moves in his body but he lives in a world of ideas. In the midst of these he experiences his greatest joys and suffers his most excruiating pains. If he allows himself to become preoccupied with small ideas, limited concepts, and petty thinking, his life becomes diminutive as an inevitable consequence. If, on the other hand, he grapples with great ideas, makes friends of magnificent concepts, and insists upon thinking on high levels, he becomes an intimate friend of the eternals.

To inquire concerning our ideas is to go more directly to the heart of life than to invoice our possessions or to take stock of our social standing. To be asked, "What's your big idea?" is to be compelled to examine the very foundations of life.

I. Life Is So Daily

A very shrewd little old lady, discussing her problems one day with Bishop Bruce Baxter, said, "The trouble with life is that it is so daily."

Trifles have such an unfortunate way of usurping our

days, sapping our strength, absorbing our interests, and forcing themselves in upon our minds. We are the daily victims of so much routine, such deadly monotony, and so many inevitables. A young businessman, having made a careful survey of his day and having listed his responsibilities, came up with the discovery that he was free to choose for himself during only a little more than one hour out of each twenty-four. "The girls who work for me," said the manager of a big chain store, "live all their lives for the sake of the three hours between eight and eleven o'clock in the evening. The rest of the time they spend on a treadmill."

Modern life is not only monotonous but a very great part of it is short lived. The mortality rate among song hits, best sellers, television entertainers, gadgets, movies, motors, and wisecracks is very high. The Goodwill Industries' bag is stuffed with the latest fashions of less than a year ago, the junk yards are full of the prides and joys of yesterday, and the elaborate hairdo for the party tonight is the wreck of tomorrow morning.

Not only is it true that the unimportant has become very insistent, but we allow the trivial to monopolize our time. While the druggist was wrapping up my prescription, he gestured with his head in the direction of the cosmetics counter and said, "Do you see that girl over there? She has spent almost forty minutes picking out some nail polish. She might have been filling her pretty little head with some great ideas, but all she has to show for the last half-hour will be ten fingernails of a slightly different color.

The inconsequential keeps us in such a hurry that we suffer exhaustion trying to outrun the petty. We have almost lost the ability to distinguish between the infinite and the infinitesimal. Radio gossip programs are timed to one-quarter of a second; we spend millions for cutoffs that shorten the driving time by half minutes; we drive at eighty-five miles

116

an hour to get nowhere in particular without seeing anything en route.

Never, perhaps, in all the history of mankind has the diminutive assumed such huge proportions. A television program offers $64,000 to the person who can answer correctly a series of questions concerning the Bible, not one of which is designed to bring any great truth forth from its pages. What wonders could be worked with the same funds if they should happen to fall into the hands of the archaeologists! The moving-picture industry spends millions in producing a spectacle which, it is frankly confessed, "is aimed at the twelve-year-old mind." Or, as one producer said with complete cynicism, "at those who are morons or studying to be morons."

One of the major responsibilities of the Christian church today is to seize modern society by the arm and shout into its ear, "What's the big idea?"

II. One Idea a Day

Life would be redeemed for millions of us moderns if we could be persuaded in some way really to wrestle with one great idea each day. It would not be necessary to explore it fully; but if it could be shown genuine hospitality within our minds for a single span of thirty minutes, it might have the effect of transforming the entire day, and eventually might transform our lives.

One unforgettable morning I was being entertained as a guest in the home of a prosperous businessman of Kyoto, Japan. My host was a person with a cultivated artistic sense as well as being a highly successful merchant. As he showed me about the house, I was so struck by a particularly beautiful vase which occupied a niche in the wall of the living room that I made some comment concerning it.

"Yes," my friend explained, "that is a way we have in

117

Japan. The first thing in the morning we enshrine some beautiful thing in that niche, and it becomes for us an object of affection for our meditation throughout the day. We gather our family about it, and in its presence we meditate. We find it makes our day beautiful to begin it with thoughts of beauty; all day long it continues with us, shedding beauty everywhere."

A quiet-mannered man appeared at the church one morning, his face aglow with happiness. When the pastor commented on his happy expression, the old gentleman said, "Yes, when I awoke this morning, I began my day by thinking a great thought about God. It was so wonderful that I have not gotten away from it. I am sure it will go with me until night comes."

A bank clerk returned to his home and his wife one evening. As he sat down at the dinner table, he said, "Let's talk about something really significant this evening. I have been thinking about nothing but money, columns of figures, and deposit slips, all day. I would like to rest my mind on something really important before I go to bed tonight."

There is a popular saying to the effect that an apple a day will keep the doctor away. Whether or not the doctors would endorse the apple rule, they would at least agree that one great idea a day will be sufficient to keep boredom away. When they advise "a change" for their patients, it is with the hope that a new environment or a change of scenery will introduce them to a new set of faces, new circumstances, and new ideas. The man who goes to a different climate and carries all his old triviality with him is wasting his money, for he will show no improvement. There can be no real recovery of either mind or spirit until we have contrived to escape from pettiness and live like children of God according to the pattern for which we were designed by our Creator.

III. Four Redemptive Ideas

There is an old story to the effect that Daniel Webster was once asked to tell the greatest idea that had ever dawned upon his consciousness. "The fact that I must someday stand before almighty God and render unto him an account of my life," the famous statesman is said to have replied.

The story may be apocryphal, but the reply is worthy of Mr. Webster. The greatest thought that ever occupies the mind of any man is related in some way to the idea of an eternal God of justice, morals, and mercy. In searching our minds for great redemptive ideas which may be expected to rescue us from triviality, let us turn our thinking in the direction of God. As a beginning, let us consider four such ideas.

1. The majesty of God. On the wall of the reception hall which circles the great Palomar telescope there hangs a series of pictures depicting various constellations and "fire mists," of which photographs have been made with the aid of the giant instrument. One of them is a pictorial representation of a "suburb of our universe" which the astronomers estimate to be 400,000,000 light-years distant. Viewing the exhibit and the inscriptions, one is left just a bit dizzy because of the inconceivable distances involved. If that were all there was to be seen or said, however, a man would perhaps be justified in deciding that he is nothing more than the most insignificant speck of dust in such an immensity. There is, however, something in the concept of infinity that stretches the mind of anyone who is willing to think seriously.

If stellar distances have the effect of leaving us with a sense of dwarfishness, let us turn for a moment to the question of age. The traditional span of a man's life is "threescore years and ten," although modern medicine and other factors seem to be lengthening it a bit of late. The anthropologists, groping their way through the misty past, guided by fossils and other queer landmarks, are now estimating that man as a self-conscious being has inhabited this earth for as much as ten thousand years with primitive man antedating him by perhaps another twenty thousand years. In contrast, the astronomers and geologists fix the age of our planet at about 4,000,000,000 years which would indicate that the Creator was at work on man's dwelling place for a considerable length of time before the tenants put in an appearance.

Government instruments atop a Kansas courthouse indicated that a full inch of water had fallen during a rain that had covered the western half of the state, bringing life and nourishment to the thirsty land and the anxious farmers. A newspaper editor, commenting on the blessings it had brought, reminded his readers that the 25,600,000 acres had been watered with 11.3 tons to the acre, which meant that God had transported 289,280,000 tons of water all the way from the Pacific Ocean, a distance of at least 2,000 miles. This, he calculated, was the equivalent of 14,464,000 tank carloads of 50 tons each. One hundred such cars would make a train approximately one mile long, and the total would require 144,640 trains. Not a bad day's work, even for God! And that stupendous total made no allowance for the rain that spilled over on Nebraska, Colorado, and Oklahoma.

When the editor began computing the heat that had been used in vaporizing all that water at sea level and the horsepower that had been expended in transporting the enormous load across the Rocky Mountains, even his linotype threatened to run out of ciphers.

Let anyone who has become just a little bored with life meditate for a few minutes on the meaning of such a universe spread out in all directions around us, and let him further consider the dimensions and power that such figures represent. Then let him further remind himself that that they are but one illustration picked at random to show the boundlessness of the universe. When we descry back of them the figure of God, the author of it all, his greatness appears truly "broader than the measure of man's mind."

2. *God and the Infinitesimal.* Such facts and figures as these with which we have been dealing have the effect of overwhelming us, so that perhaps we can be excused for feeling it is impossible for men to lay claim to any importance in such a universe. Any person experiencing such sensations of inferiority may well pause and get a glimpse of the universes that lie under his feet. Those universes will appear immediately to be as fascinating and as awe-inspiring as those over our heads.

Let us, then, pass for a moment from a consideration of the infinite to a contemplation of the opposite—the infinitesimal. The chemists tells us, for example, that when we look at a liquid we do not actually see it. In fact, no one has ever actually seen it under the most powerful magnifying glass, for it really consists of an inconceivably numerous collection of molecules—each one of which is so small that it eludes the most perfect lens ever made. A teaspoonful of water, they tell us, consists of a mere 500,000,000,000,000,-000,000,000 molecules, and each molecule consists of two atoms of hydrogen and one of oxygen. Then, as if that were not reducing the matter sufficiently, they go on to explain that each atom, if it were sufficiently magnified, would have the appearance of being a swarm of 200,000 bees buzzing about in a room ten feet square, each bee flying at the speed of 1,500 feet per second!

Under a microscope, a gram of earth is seen to be filled with literally millions of living organisms. Similarly, the air we breathe is composed of billions of atoms to the cubic centimeter of the various component gases. Under a lens sufficiently powerful, every solid substance would be seen to be porous. An empty bottle, made of fine glass and hermetically sealed, if dropped to the bottom of the sea will be found to contain water when it is drawn up to the surface, for the terrific pressure which is registered at the floor of the ocean is sufficient to force molecules of water through the glass, between the molecules of silica of which the bottle is composed. Even a cubic inch of "vacuum" is said by the scientists to contain literally billions of atmospheric atoms. Again, so minute are the bacteria which cause rabies that no scientist has ever been able to devise a filter fine enough to isolate them from their surrounding solution.

Something of the beauty and perfection of the worlds under our feet appears when we examine a little woods violet, for example, under a high-powered microscope. The cellular structure, the delicacy of design, and the amazing efficiency of the plant never fail to command the profound respect of the first-time viewer, an admiration that continues to grow as the exploration continues.

There is a story told of an old Scotch farmer who looked at a little wild flower under a microscope one day for the first time. Its amazing beauty and its astonishing construction awed him into silence. Finally, when he recovered his speech, he said very solemnly, "If I had ever known it was so beautiful I would never have stepped on it!"

Henshaw Ward in his *Exploring the Universe* is awed by the complex structure of a tree. He tells of a Torrey Pine—the trunk of the tree nearly one hundred feet in height, and the branches nearly one hundred feet in spread. Viewed from a distance the tree is a soft grey-green cloud of foliage; seen from below, it is a veritable galaxy of slender eight-inch needles. The trunk of the tree, almost four feet in diameter, is a notable achievement in architecture and construction. Amid the wildest gale it can carry the heavy load laid on it.

The branches of the tree? They are contrived in such a way that they expose thousands of needles to the sun and air, and so enable the needles to manufacture sugar to feed new twigs which in turn produce new needles. The roots of the tree? They reach out in every direction and dwindle to the dimensions of rootlets, and then the rootlets dwindle until they become fine hairs. The roots and the rootlets forage for the water and the mineral food needed by the thousands of needles far above.

Suppose you were reduced in size until you became only one thirty-thousandth of an inch tall—about the size of one of the smallest bacteria. This would mean that you could make your way comfortably into the root of the tree, and then on into a rootlet, finally into one of the hairs growing out of the rootlet. Thus you would finally reach one of the outposts of the tree. There the outermost cell of the hair in which you are standing is wrestling with a bit of loam which has in its possession a few molecules of water. The cell gathers the loam in its embrace, and by a process no one quite understands, abstracts the water from the loam. Then the cell conveys the water from its outer surface to its inner side and pushes the water against the wall of the adjacent cell. So the water is passed from cell to cell, and thus it goes back and up through the hair to the root of the tree. Reaching the tree, it is somehow lifted to the thirsty needles one hundred feet above. How the tree lifts the water this distance is a riddle which even the most painstaking studies of physicists have failed to solve. [1]

Even such a brief excursion into the universe of the infinitesimal makes it plain that man stands at some point midway between the universes that spread out under his feet

[1] Retold from pp. 97-124. Copyright 1927, 1954, and used by special permission of the publishers, The Bobbs-Merrill Co., Inc.

and that which covers him above. Let no man feel discouraged over the fact that he seems small in comparison with stellar spaces. Let him consider rather how vast he must seem to atoms and molecules!

3. *The Patience of God.* If the geologists are even approximately correct in their estimate of the age of the planet— 4,000,000,000 years—the human lifespan of seventy years is no more than the most minute fraction of the total of time. If, inside that relatively infinitesimal period we are in danger of growing impatient, let us try to get a glimpse of the patience of God.

Stand if you will at the edge of the Grand Canyon of Arizona and try to pick out the silvery ribbon which is the Colorado River, more than five thousand feet below. Stretch your mind and strain your eyes across the tremendous chasm to the rim on the opposite side miles away. Then meditate on the fact that the entire spectacle represents the achievement of that slender engraving tool of water in the hands of an infinite God working through millennia. Millions of years before any of our troubles ever began to occur, God started digging the canyon, and long after our troubles are all over, he will doubtless still be at it.

One Old Testament writer thus admonishes us: "Be still, and know that I am God." It would be appropriate for the modern geologist to say to all impatient folk, "Wait ten million years and you will know much more than you do now."

Let any man who is growing nervous and tense because he cannot see the signs of the triumph of righteousness consider the patience of God for twenty minutes each day for a week. He will be amazed at the spirit of serenity that will begin to creep in upon his whole life. The redemptive power of an idea so big is almost beyond our power to compute.

4. The love of God. The fourth great thought to which the nervous, the anxious, and the fearful are commended is the inalienable solicitude of God for his children. And the sight to which our attention is invariably directed is a cross just outside a city wall, upon which cross Jesus of Nazareth hangs, dying, and praying all the time, "Father, forgive them; for they know not what they do."

The hymn writer gave the idea dramatic expression when he wrote:

> Two wonders I confess:
> The wonders of redeeming love
> And my unworthiness.

Years ago I heard the story of a terrible night when, in the midst of a raging storm, a little ship was seen foundering a few hundred yards offshore from a small New England fishing village. At the height of the storm, when it was seen to be breaking up, the vicar of the tiny church on the side of the hill plunged into the sea and, after a terrific struggle, managed to bring back the drunken old sea captain. In doing so, however, the young minister was badly beaten on the rocks and, as he lay dying on the dock, the grizzled old sailor knelt at his side sobbing and saying, "But, domine, why did you do it? I'm not worth it!" Whereupon the clergyman gasped, "Then *be* worth it!"

There is enough in the picture of the cross and of the dying young vicar to occupy the mind of any sensitive spirit for the rest of the man's natural life!

Let any man who has found life going stale on his hands— who has found strange questions tormenting his mind—take time to hold twenty minutes' communion with any one of these four great ideas, once every day. Within the space of no more than a few weeks, he will discover that a new spirit has taken possession of him.

Redemption will have taken place because he has substituted a big idea for many small ones.

How big is the biggest idea with which you have been occupied during the last twenty-four hours?